Inside the DARK UNDERBELLY OF RIKERS ISLAND

A RETIRED FEMALE CORRECTION OFFICER SPEAKS OUT

ROBIN K. MILLER

DEDICATION

I dedicate this book to my big sister and only sibling, Theresa, whose choice to become a New York City Correction Officer at my recommendation and encouragement ultimately cost her her life. After watching her struggle with three jobs in order to support her son, my nephew Delamar, I believed in my heart that my recommendation would make her life, and his, much easier.

The last time I saw her on July 1, 2005, my official retirement date. Ironically, her life ended on July 2. She had come to my house earlier, begging me to make sure that I would never abandon Delamar who was at the time in jail, fighting for his freedom. To this day, I honor that promise. She, tragically, had fallen prey to the dark underbelly of drug trafficking among certain correction officers, and the crack cocaine use soon led to illness, that eventually led to her death. I will always feel partially responsible because of the encouragement I gave her to join "the good guys".

May this book, my story, expose what is corrupt and help save others. May I become their impassioned voice.

PROLOGUE

Part of Robin K Miller is still locked up inside Rikers Island, along with the spirit of her deceased sister. The current upheavals and violence taking place in and around the infamous Island are also taking place inside Robin's tortured heart.

A correction guard at Rikers Island for 20 years, Robin's story is not merely a bold and brave expose of what really happens "behind closed doors", it is the deeply intimate and wrenching odyssey of a woman who has survived the un-survivable, and who is committed to sharing her truth. Her story is the ultimate triumph over darkness and corruption.

The other story is that of an institution riddled with decay and corruption. Together theirs form a strident call to action for the entire American penal system.

CONTENTS

ACKNOWLEDGMENTS

I thank the Almighty God because he has shown me with him all things are possible. I would like to express my gratitude to everyone took an interest in my story and encouraged me to move forward.

I would like to thank Gary Buiso from the New York Post. It was your phenomenal journalism that put me on the map and made people pay attention. You gave me a Sunday Edition two-page spread and this article allowed me to get everyone's attention and present my book to the world. You are a great journalist and I expect to see big things from you in the future.

I would like to thank Sarina Trangle formerly from the Queens Times Ledger. You were the first person to interview me and it was your interview that unlocked the pain I had hidden for so many years of the abuse I endured as a Correction Officer.

I would like to thank Pinedo Anstides and the producer from ABC NIGHTLINE NEWS for the interview, you were patience and professional. I love you guys.

CNN's Anderson Cooper 360, Producer Elise Miller and the makeup crew and staff for making me feel like a million bucks. Anderson Cooper you are the best in the business and I was honored to be in your presence, CNN Poppy Harlow and Editorial Producer Halayne Ehrenberg thank you for the great interview and allowing me to sit beside greatness. Poppy Harlow you are a class act.

I would like to thank my daughter Jeanine, for loving me and holding my hand post retirement. Your determination to excel in life brightens my heart. When I look at you, I know I did something right in life. You have and will always be the sunshine of my life.

To my dad. Thank you for just being my dad and loving me unconditionally. I love you so much and hope I you are proud.

To my nephew Delamar Brown. I thank you for making me smile in spite of your circumstances. Your encouragement and support has made me move full steam ahead.

To Civil Rights Attorney Norman Siegel, thank you for gracing the back of my book with your kind words and opening your heart and doors to me and my cause.

You are such an amazing man and inspiration to me. No matter how busy you are. You always find a little time for me and for that I am so grateful.

To My Angel and Agent Nancy Ellis from Nancy Ellis Literary Agency. Thank you for holding my hand, loving and listening to me. You didn't know me from a can of paint and believed in my story, me and edited my book from the kindness of your heart, to enable me to release a polished product to the world. I love you so much.

To Artyom Matusov thank you for being a dear friend and kind spirit. You believed in me and helped me so much, even when the naysayers said it wasn't going to happen.

You've had my back from the very beginning for nothing in return. It was your persistence that prompted Norman Siegel to connect with me. I owe you so much and I will never forget it. I love you for life.

To Rob Klein my amazing photographer with a golden eye and took superb photos for my book cover. You are definitely the best in the business and have such a warm spirit. Thank you for the beautiful pictures and marvelous photo shoot.

To my amazing makeup artist Sharelle D. FeQuiere , you are a gifted talented make-up artist. You are so professional, beautiful and patient. I look forward to our road ahead.

A special thanks to Dimitrinka Cvetkoski - Peacock Design, for the wonderful book cover design and inside book design. You are amazing, professional and talented. You completed this work in less than a week. I am very appreciative of your work and glad I found you on the www.fiverr.com/peacockdesign site.

To Raymond Davis Jr. thank you for being my biggest supporter and never giving up on me. You kind words and encouragement has meant the word to me.

To my best friend Jovanka (Joanne) Radivojevic. You had my back when everyone turned their backs on me. I will be forever grateful. Thank you for truly being my friend.

INTRODUCTION

Before you begin reading this book, I want to emphatically state that this book does not reflect every city and state correction officer and superior officers, just a small minority. However, it is that small minority in the city and state correction department, that is giving the correction officers overall a terrible reputation.

I did not work with every correction officer or work in every jail. It is important to me that I address that. The damaging truths I do reveal are significant , and the American public needs to know. I do name names, real names: Ex-Commissioner Bernard Kerik , my relationship with Chief of Corrections Eric M Taylor, Warden's. Correction Officers, NYS Greenhaven Correctional Facility's Superintendent Griffin, Deputy Superintendent Collado, Captain Daniel Cary and many more.

There is a war being waged here in New York City and people are dying at the hands of the police of the streets and the police of the jails. If things do not change in the prison system with the major outbreak of prison abuse by New York City and State Correction Officers, it's only a matter of time before the prison inmates start fighting back in the form of riots. The prisons here in New York City and New York State will be taken over by inmates.

There are too many unjustifiable deaths and injuries going unreported or cover-ups by the correction department, and Albany is doing nothing about it. Some New York State Correction Officers in Greenhaven Correctional Facility are worse than the Correction Officers on Rikers Island that I worked with. While I hear that state prison abuse is rampant , I can only vouch for Greenhaven Correctional Facility because they beat my nephew to a pulp in 2014.

No one is focusing on the state prisons, but it's about time they do. The same thing that is going on in Rikers Island is going on in the upstate prisons, only worse. There is no watch dog penalizing the corrupt correction officers. They are given stripes and being rewarded for "dismantling" an inmate. This has to stop.

The Correction Officers I worked with made my life a living hell. If they treat one of their own like crap, imagine what they will do to you.

I started this job fresh out of high school. I was able to function and relate because I grew up in the Brownsville Housing projects in Brooklyn, and many of the faces of the prisoners I saw in jail, were recognizable and their behavior, I could identify with.

Jail is not corporate America, even though corporate America has its financial business hands in it. Jail is an ugly, negative environment that is holding people rightfully or wrongfully against their will. It is an art to deal with a black person, who is highly intelligent, and also commits criminal acts. The reason I say black person is because , corporate America has made a business out of jailing young black men.

People's rights are violated everyday, I know that personally because my nephew Delamar Brown was almost killed by the guards in New York State Greenhaven Correctional facility, for no reason other than I think is me writing this book. I would like to see them charged with attempted murder.

I will show throughout the book how my generation of correction officers in the 80's constructed the blueprint for demise of the correction department today.

There is a light at the end of the tunnel. I do offer glimmers of hope for a brighter future within the New York City and New York State prison system. Welcome to an unimaginable but very real "dark world"

CHAPTER 1

THE TRUTH SHALL SET YOU FREE

I worked as a female correction officer in a male dominated atmosphere from 1983-2005, when I retired I decided to initially write this book for two reasons. One, because I was physically abused as a rookie Correction Officer in 1984 by a 6'4 250lb black, male Correction Officer James Carter. He physically attacked me while I was working on a Rikers Island gate area after we had exchanged words. This assault left me bloody, and with a fractured finger. For over 28 years I blocked the entire incident out.

It wasn't until I was asked by reporter Sarina Trangle from the Queens Times Ledger newspaper, for proof that I had worked on Rikers Island from 1983-1984. I went through my archive of important documents and discovered this ripe old age report still intact. At that moment I mentally relived the entire ordeal all over again. As I read the legal document I submitted to Warden Bains, I discovered that not only was I assaulted but it was covered up by the administration. I was penalized (had to work 3 days for free) and it followed me my whole career. Correction Officer James Carter should have been arrested and fired.

That was just the beginning. As I continued to read, I began to feel anxiety regarding all the other abuses inflicted upon me, by other colleagues throughout my entire career.

I was also pushed down the stairs in my home by a male correction officer I used to date, and attacked by him again years later. I still have the physical scars on my shoulder to prove it. This guy made it to the rank of captain and retired with a hefty pension. I never reported it and continued to date him for several years after that, like an ass. That was the last "piece of shit officer" that put their hands on me. That same correction officer attacked a colleague and his spouse "impregnated both" by punching the colleague in the stomach, she miscarried, and the spouse had the baby and divorced him. I personally spoke to them.

Before he retired he dated a colleague and abused her too. When she decided to leave him, he made her life a living hell and tried to make her lose her job. I also know there are other female Correction Officers who have been or are battered women in the system, all by male correction employees. They do not have an outlet to complain, nor do they have protection.

Men run the correction department. Many male correction officers act like pimps and treat female officers worst than you would treat a prostitute. These women are afraid to come forth because most likely nothing will happen.

My second reason for writing this book is because of my sister Theresa Miller whom I helped obtain this job as a Correction Officer. She went through the entire process, passed every exam and they would not hire her. I interceded and made a call and she was hired. My sister's life went downhill after she became a Correction Officer. This job was supposed to elevate her financially, so she could give herself and my nephew a great life. Instead it made her life a nightmare.

My sister wasn't the social type and became an outcast because of that. To fit in she began to hang out with some of the officers, and then she was targeted by this particular drug dealing Correction Officer to buy drugs. She eventually became addicted to crack-cocaine, quit her job, prostituted to support her crack habit , served time in jail, then while in prison she learned she had HIV, lost custody of her son, fixed her life, regained custody, relapse after relapse, eventually went on dialysis 3 times a week and then she was dead. I found out from my aunt, at my sister's funeral, how much she hated the job and I could only imagine what she went through, because I knew how the Correction Officers made my life a living hell.

I watched her battle her crack addiction for over 20 years and I always felt a certain amount of guilt because I helped her get the job, so she could take care of my nephew. I know it's not my fault that she chose to do drugs. I just have a problem because this addictive drug was introduced to her by a male Correction Officer, who took an oath to serve and protect.

In order for me to work and survive there amongst primarily male street criminals, I had to speak their language and be quick on my feet.

To be successful at being a correction officer, you have to tap into an inmate's mindset and assess his demeanor at all times because you will spend the majority of your career, in direct contact with inmates. The sad thing about my tenure there was that, I rarely had problems with inmates. It was always my colleagues derailing our purpose there. That is not what I signed up for. Correction Officers will gang up on a co-worker in a minute, if they are not part of their circle. I was never part of anyone's circle. To me there is no difference from the bloods and crips and correction officers. Correction Officers are the biggest gang in the world. You hear all about police brutality, but rarely about the correction officer brutality.

My book does not focus on just one year (1983), its about my entire career which is also part of the history of the correction department. I retired in 2005.

A large portion of the general public has no idea what an inmate is. Society has you believing that anyone locked up is guilty, deserving whatever happens. What you fail to realize is we are all a hop, skip and a jump from being arrested for anything, innocent or guilty. Someone can lie on you or set you up. Or you can be placed into a situation where you have to defend yourself. An allegation can send you to Rikers Island to prove your innocence. At that point you will be "taken care of" by some of the most notorious Correction Officers that I worked with.

You are about to enter my world, the world I ultimately escaped from. Reader enter that world with trepidation.

CHAPTER 2

WHAT IS A CORRECTION OFFICER?

I was a New York City Correction Officer for 20 years. I think I am in the position to give you my up close and personal expert opinion of what a correction officer is. I have worked around and with numerous correction officers throughout my career. There are many great officers, who make a difference in the reformation of prisoners who enter the prison system. There are , however, some correction officers who are so corrupt they give correction officers a bad name. It becomes embarrassing to admit that is what you do for a living.

Looking back now, it is partly because of these bad apples that I regret ever becoming a correction officer. I wish I would have chosen a different profession. Do not get me wrong, I am grateful for the job. I was able to live a better life than most, but now it feels more like blood money.

In this chapter, I will give my assessment of the good, the bad and the ugly of what a correction officer is supposed to be, and what transformational Correction Officer character you might encounter. God forbid you, your family or friends are ever arrested.

THE GOOD:

What is a Correction Officer ? Rikers Island Correction Officers are responsible for the care, custody and control of individuals who have been arrested, and are awaiting trial, or who have been convicted of a crime and sentenced to serve time in jail. They are also responsible for the safety and security of the facility itself.

A Correction Officer, often referred to as a guard, C.O., babysitter, high paid nannies, security guard, jail guard and police of the jails. The bottom line is we watch prisoners all day. The model definition is CARE, CUSTODY and CONTROL of inmates: cut and dry.

In the early 80's starting pay was $21,000 a year climbing to $27,000 after 3 years. That was a lot of money back then. The benefits were free medical, optical, dental and with paid holidays, uniform allowance and 5 weeks paid vacation, plus unlimited sick leave. The current pay has escalated and some NYC Correction Officers are making close to $100,000 a year. I would assume most people take the test because they are attracted to the money. Living in New York City is expensive, and the bottom line is you need a good job to be able to afford to live comfortably in NYC. A Correction Officer's salary places them in an upper middle class range. With a salary like that and the power we posses, we should be some happy campers. We should appreciate going to work everyday and be extremely thankful to be so fortunate.

Yes, being a Correction Officer can be financially rewarding and commendations should be in order because of what we are exposed to, on a daily basis. The average Joe or Jane could not handle some of these horrible misfits and criminals. The environment is hazardous and our job is not easy . We are in the line of fire every moment because we are outnumbered in a prison setting. For every Correction Officer there are over 100 inmates. However this is what we signed up for, so there is no need to complain and we are paid handsomely to do the grubby work.

THE BAD:

Do people look down on us? Yes! Correction Officers are treated like second-class citizens, and looked down on, as is we are inmates: the very alleged criminals we are hired to watch. To a degree, the media has tainted the portrayal of a Correction Officer. Furthermore, the public's perception is that correction officers, and inmates are one of the same. At the same time, the recent headlines of corruption did not help paint a brighter picture. In all actuality, this is nothing new. We as Correction Officers know exactly what goes on, in the inside whether we want to admit it publicly or not. We hide behind the blue cement wall and crucify anyone for speaking out.

No one is excited to become a Correction Officer. When you ask a child what they want to be when they grow up. They never say, "I want to be a Correction Officer", maybe a police officer, but never a correction officer.

Correction Officers have the same badge, gun, uniform, salary and benefits as the police officers. The police, police the streets. Correction Officers polices the jails. We do not get the respect or recognition we deserve. I think a Correction Officer's job is harder.

The correction department considered a quasi-military establishment. Trained in low-level martial arts, CPR , communication skills and report writing among-st many forms of training we receive at the training academy that I attended in 1983 for 8 weeks . The training does not prepare you for what you are about to experience when you enter the prison system, surrounded by alleged criminals all day in a prison setting and baby-sitting possibly some of the worst misfits in society. A Rikers Island Correction Officer does not carry a weapon inside the jails because we are outnumbered. A prisoner can grab our weapon and do some serious damage. It is a dangerous job and we have to rely on our communication skills in order to survive.

The Rikers Island prisoners rely solely on us for everything, from soap, toilet paper, food, medical attention, protection to church service escorting. As a Correction Officer at times, you unknowingly assume the role of grandparents, parents, siblings, aunts, uncles, psychiatrist and for some boyfriend and girlfriend.

I honestly believe if many of the Correction Officers on Rikers island focused on correcting and reforming back in the 80's . The streets of New York City would be a lot safer today. Why? Prisoners released from the prison system in the 80's & 90's, that were exposed to consistent forms of corruption, verbal and physical abuse by Correction Officers, took that anger and mindset, back to the streets. The streets are a mirror image of the jail system. There used to be fewer weapons in jail. I beg to differ now.

It is extremely difficult to defend and make good arguments for city correction officers that are abusive and disrespectful to whomever they encounter, primarily, because the New York City Department of Corrections is at fault with their training approach from the very beginning of the officer's career. It is negative, abusive and full of discrimination on every level. They feed us red meat and venom from the door and place a negative tone on how we should present ourselves to Rikers Island prisoners. It's as simple as raising and teaching a baby. You give them the blueprint and they will follow it. The same thing applies to the new recruit correction officer. You give them the blueprint and they will follow it. That will be the norm.

Let me take it another step further and give you an example: A baby does not come out of the womb a racist. They are taught racial discrimination from their parents at an early age and will apply it. Therefore when newly hired correction officers are brainwashed and abusive seeds are planted by academy instructors, programming them to believe that a Rikers Island prisoner, "mind you has only been accused of a crime, not convicted" is an animal, the enemy, scumbag and extremely dangerous. The prejudgment is a set up for failure. They are entering the lion's den as if they are at the Iraq war. Utilizing Guantanamo Bay tactics, on prisoners who have yet to have their day in court. That is a recipe for disaster. I do understand that some prisoners are extremely dangerous and act like untamed animals, not all are. You have at least 50% of prisoners that are victims of circumstances.

What a Correction Officer is supposed to be and the reality of what it is: is contradictory. A Correction Officer has the power to make a powerful difference in prisoners mindset and contribution to reforming the system. I think we made it worse by further scarring them, with our own idiosyncrasies, personal issues and NYCDOC training.

You have to understand something. When I was hired, most people were in their twenties and still kids themselves. We were a couple of years shy of a teenager, a little wet behind the ears. Subsequently you dress us up in a blue police uniform, give us a badge and if they score 65-70% percent at the gun range, you give us a gun, with a bunch of rules to follow. We are now of a big gang organization with an abusive agenda of keeping prisoners in line by beating and punishing them. This is before they graduate out of the academy. That might be too much power and confusion for any teenager/young adult to handle. Most individuals are not mature enough to live on their own or best yet make good sound decisions. The majority of the Correction Officers were sent to Rikers Island, to work directly with prisoners, after they completed their training and graduated from the correction academy, with the exception of those who had family members or knee-pad clout in the Commissioners office.

Rikers Island is where it all begins for a spanking new correction officer. Meanwhile you are putting us in charge of grown men and women incarcerated on Rikers Island.

There is a great deal of Correction Officers that could handle that type of power. However, unfortunately , many could not and today's headlines are the aftermath of generations passing torches of corruption and misconduct to the newcomer, new jack or rookie. Scores of rookies' goals are to impress and please senior and superior officers. They become highly influenced by their senior officers, and work hard applying what they learned to fit in. Reform is definitely out of the question. Therefore, if you are not training the new recruits to properly utilize their communication skills. What in the world, do you expect?

THE UGLY:

A Correction Officer is supposed to carry himself or herself in a professional manner at all times. That is a bunch of bullshit because many of my colleagues are some nasty, bitter, miserable, mean people and undeserving of the job. Ask any civilian or outside agency about the treatment they received when visiting a correctional facility.

Some of these Correction Officers are crazy when they come on the job. They have so many family and personal issues they have not dealt with. Instead of them embracing the great opportunity of having a good job, they create toxicity around them. They are angry, extremely dark and filled with hatred. The department know these individuals are crazy and they cover for them. They are a ticking time bomb and thrive off beating prisoners. When you train a person with this type of demeanor that the prisoner is the enemy. You give them a license to institute violence and it will become excessive at times. If you are mentally unstable, you have no business applying for any law enforcement job.

There was a shortage of correction officers in the early eighties and the hiring process was quick. I went through the entire process in six months. I mean I took my written exam, physical, background check, psychological and medical. **Boom, boom and boom ! HIRED !** Thank God I was not crazy, then again maybe I was.

They hired any and everybody. That was definitely a big mistake. The drug and psychological screening was juvenile. Countless Correction Officers came on the job with violent tendencies and using drugs. Their drug use escalated.

Some Correction Officers cannot deal with the stresses of the job and use drugs and alcohol to cope. Most Correction Officers, active and retired are bonafide alcoholics and either do not realize, or refuse to admit it, until its too late. It is common practice to go to the bar after every tour of duty. It gets to the point they need alcohol to cope. Eventually they start getting drunk at work and that is a recipe for disaster. They begin looking for a prisoner to beat down. I call it liquid courage for the coward.

A Correction Officer's drug and alcohol addiction is detrimental to any environment. They place themselves in a compromised position and become one of the primary sources of drug and weapon smuggling. Endangering the lives, safety and security of, first and foremost their colleagues. You do one favor for a prisoner and he owns you and will turn on you like a pit bull, after you have done their dirty work.

On Rikers Island Correction Officers needs to discontinue the process of playing judge and jury towards prisoners. They are two-steps shy of walking out the door. They have only been accused of a crime, so why are they an automatic scumbag. We are not supposed to verbally abuse nor provoke them into an incident so we can justify a beat down, and beat prisoners to a pulp, and write false reports against prisoners. The title, badge and gun does not give any Correction Officer a license to attempt murder or perform gang style beatings on a prisoner, because when you brutally beat a prisoner who is not fighting back. You are committing a crime and undeserving of the job.

In the early eighties, we used to carry a long black heavy metal flashlights and many correction officers took it upon themselves to use that as a lethal weapon. I witnessed many unprovoked flashlight torturous beatings by many of my senior colleagues, sending many prisoners to the hospital, forcing the department to ban long metal flashlights.

Look at it this way, I started in 1983 and witnessed this type of behavior from the inside, until I retired. The only difference between what was going on then and what is going on now is the correction officers and media did not report it. The mental state of any correction officer, is the driving force to how they perform their role and duties and what they condone and what they will report.

As far as I am concerned, the psychological test is the most important part of hiring any law enforcement officer. How they function and conduct themselves, in society, is a major factor with their upbringing. Their morals, integrity, and standards taught to them during their early childhood can play a major part in the communication and people skills. Cases in point.

If raised in a violent abusive household, whether it is their own or foster care, visual, violent behavior becomes the norm. Therefore, it is nothing for them to become extremely violent at work. This constitutes the loose cannon correction officers.

If their parents were lazy and kept, a dirty house and they was that lazy ass child that never cleaned their room. They will most likely be that lazy ass officer that never keeps their work area clean and the jail housing areas they worked in will be filthy and dirty too. My colleagues know exactly who these nasty ass officers were.

If they did not listen to their parents and had their own set of rules, there is a great chance, they will disrespect their superior officers, making their own rules, and are more apt to be that abusive drug-dealing officer.

If you hire a female and she spent most of her teenage years sexually abused or whoring around, or neglected by her father, she will more likely than not have sex with a prisoner. They call it looking for love in all the wrong places, and needing male acceptance, possibly seeking attention they never got from their fathers. I equate that to low self esteem and the male prisoners notice that. They give these type of female officers extra attention and compliments. Some of these female officers are so smitten by these prisoners, they will bring any and everything these prisoners desire. If they can smuggle in the Brooklyn Bridge unnoticed, they'd bring that in too.

NYCDOC had a low standard regarding the hiring process in the early eighties. They did not fully screen their candidates and still do not. They really had no idea what and whom they were putting in charge in a supervisory position then and now. Correction Officers are supervisors of prisoners. That's a big responsibility.

If their **MINDSET** is on point, they can really have a positive impact on a prisoner's life. Reformation at the highest level is the greatest achievement. If each Correction Officer can take a couple of prisoners under their wings, whether they are recidivist or first timers. The prison system might be a better environment if a Correction Officer would utilize their communication skills to alter a prisoner's thought process concerning their outlook on life. They may deter maybe one prisoner from a life of crime.

What I never understood is our job description is "care, custody and control", and in order to do that, you have to communicate with prisoners. You have to tap into the **MINDSET** of a prisoner and figure out their capabilities. However, there are Correction Officers who shun the idea of conversing with a prisoner and shun officers who institute their job description. They are labeled inmate lover if they show any concern about a prisoners well being.

As a female officer who worked primarily in a male jail or with male prisoners my entire career. It is imperative to utilize the psychological approach. A woman does not have the physical capabilities to go toe to toe with a male prisoner. It is as simple as that. The same way prisoners study us, we have to study them and try to figure out what they are capable of, and how to persuade them to cooperate with the process. That is how I survived 20 years as a Correction Officer. I was able to tap into their psyche, just by doing my job. I kept it real and demanded respect. I also gave respect and tried to stray away from judging them.

It comes back to **MINDSET**. Therefore if you have a bunch of regular people with serious multiple issues and displacements, wearing a badge with enormous power in society, interacting with people in the prison system. You cannot expect glorious results.

What I want you the reader, who is in a non-uniformed force to do, is, look at or think about everyone in your immediate workplace. I do not care if it is a bank, fast food restaurant, office etc. Some of your coworkers are cool and some are idiots, some are book smart but lack common sense, lazy, gossipers, ass kissers, mean, hateful, always arriving to work late, complainers, stink, loose, whorish and backstabbers.

Now with those qualities visualize your coworkers, not naked, but with a Correction of Police Officer uniform. Picture them with badges and guns and ask yourself would you be okay if they worked in law enforcement, and if you or your family member were arrested and under their custody and supervision. Well that is it concisely and what it boils down to being a "Correction Officer"

So to sum up this what is a correction officer, I will say this, a correction officer is nothing but a high paid babysitter. The job as a correction officer although financially rewarding, it's not mentally stimulating: for me it was quite boring watching groan ass people bitch and moan all day long. However, the saying idle time is the devil's playground is part of the reason for these extra criminal curriculum activities. There is a thin line between being a correction officer and being an inmate.

There has been a "culture of violence" by Correction Officers against inmates and their colleagues. They are using force to punish or take revenge. This has to end. You cannot place total blame on the new breed of correction officers. This stuff has been going on since I joined the force in the eighties and probably prior to that. There is a serious problem now because this learned behavior is hard to break and has already taken an evil turn.

The death of a Correction Officer literally in the prison and full fledged riots resulting in multiple injuries or possibly death are inevitable.

The system needs to be reformed from the very beginning of a Correction Officer's career and sensitivity training needs to be instituted throughout their careers, as well as hidden watchdogs in the facilities. Reform can only work if both parties are respectful and safe.

CHAPTER 3

CHAIN OF COMMAND

What exactly is a chain of command? The chain of command in the New York City Department of Correction is a series of quasi-military ranks in which each has direct authority over the one immediately below. It is my opinion the ranking officers from the 80's to present are responsible, for the disarray we are in today. The written and unwritten policies instituted to maintain law and order in the jails, got out of hand. The norm of abuse and corruption is the fault of the ranking officers and their bosses, the Mayors, Commissioners and Chiefs of Operation. Why?

Plain ole failure to supervise, by allowing violence, corruption and abuse to transition from administration to each new administration. It was more about budget cutting, making it appear they had prison violence under control, and saving the city money. Whereas, reforming should have been on the forefront , it was on the backburner.

Correction Officers were not fully at fault. They did what they were taught, instructed and ordered to do. On the other hand, some went along with corruption to fit in or get along. Unfortunately many will pay the price.

In the 80's, the chain of command above the rank of correction officer on Rikers Island as well as borough jails were as follows; Captain, Assistant Deputy Warden, Warden, Supervising Warden, Chief of Operations, and Commissioner. In a jail facility, the Captain ranked lowest and Warden ranked highest. They eventually changed some of the titles above Captain to Division Chiefs.

The court facilities such as, Manhattan, Bronx, Brooklyn and Queens courts chain of command highest-ranking officer was Assistant Deputy Warden. The Warden of the borough jails was largely responsible for the court facilities.

How do you get a ranking position? You have to take a civil service exam and pass to get promoted to the rank of Captain and Assistant Deputy Warden.

To be promoted to a position above the rank of Assistant Deputy Warden, it most likely becomes the "who you know, who you blow syndrome" You have to be in some sort of inner circle. (not all the time)

The Mayor is the top dog of the correction department, no matter how you slice it. It has been common practice after every city mayoral election; the Mayor brings in his own people to run the correction department: a new administration and new agenda.

As a Correction Officer you are bombarded with a team of supervisors. Most have egos the size of a continent and walk around wearing white shirts reeking of the superiority complex, or napoleon syndrome, just looking to demean anyone below their rank. They have power and can make or break your career.

My assessment stemming from 1983-2005 during my career as a correction officer was the Mayor appoints a Commissioner and Chief of Operations to carry out his orders and how he thinks the correction department should run. They literally control the Commissioner. The Commissioner's goal is pleasing the mayor. There is no exam; so many Commissioners will do whatever the Mayor tells them to do. They want to keep their prestigious cushiony positions and salary.

They are not the least bit concerned the correction officers are overworked, understaffed and their lives are placed in jeopardy on a daily basis. Several correction officers who climbed the ranks have a convenient amnesia . They are so thirsty for the power; they leave their conscience at the door and forget what its like in the housing areas of the prison. They will throw a correction officer under the bus in a nano second.

If a Commissioner is appointed, that never worked in a jail; it could be a recipe for disaster. They have no idea what goes on inside the jail and tend to believe what they see on TV.

The Mayor's and Commissioner's moral compass will most likely determine the temperament in the jails, and how the prisoners, and Correction Officers are treated. Reason being; the prisoners' and correction officers are at the bottom of the totem pole.

*There is a **plantation/slave/master breakdown in Chapter 6 "Rikers "Hell" Island** *

Overall, the Captains are responsible for the correction officers and prisoners. The Captain answers to the Assistant Deputy Warden, who is the tour commander in every New York City jail. The goal is to continue climbing the ranks, I guarantee you there were causalities and sacrificial lambs along the way, up the jail ranking ladder.

Many of today's incarcerated are beneficiaries of imprisoned parents from the 80's throughout. Correction and ranking officers had a hand in scarring them for life with their excessive physical, mental and emotional abuse. These prisoners were discharged from the prison system and unleashed to the streets damaged, and the general public suffered because of it. The psychological damage has scarred them for life. They leave prison violent and angry

A prisoner abused on Rikers Island with the consent of, or by a ranking officer and cover-ups, is not the prescription for kumbaya and that prisoner will eventually resent authority and will strike back. Nowadays, prisoners are assaulting ranking officers too.

The ranking officers in my era encouraged it or sat back and allowed it to happen. I personally witnessed this on many occasions. Now it is difficult for any new Mayors or Commissioners to clean up this horrific mess and the Correction Officers are the casualties.

It is reminiscent of President Obama cleaning up the Bush mess, while the middle class suffered. I am extremely optimistic; this broken system is fixable.

I blame one Mayor in particular for the destruction of the correction department. It is my opinion that his blind eye, by any means necessary approach, is why the department is a mess now. He had the media and the court system in his pocket. Under his supervision, it became worse, even though on paper, it appeared he was doing a terrific job. There was a major racial divide when he took office. The prejudice among staff was always there, but it escalated to a recognizable level. White people in power started flexing their muscles and many of their subordinates or colleagues became casualties. They wanted to be the majority in charge. Abuse of power was at an all time high, roles reversed and prisoners were the lesser target.

At that time if you were a correction or ranking officer with connections to this regime, the Commissioner's or Mayor's office, that equaled enormous power. You were privy to perquisites because of those connections, which we refer to as a "hook" or "juice". If someone didn't like you and had connections. You were toast. They would blatantly make your life a living hell.

The talk amongst the minorities was, that the white people's goal was to get rid of Black and Latinos and fill those positions with white counterparts. I am not a militant, nor pulling the race card. It was what it was. It became blatantly obvious because most of the people in the direct trenches with prisoners were minority, not white. You could count the number of white officers in the housing and dorm areas, with direct prisoner contact. I wonder if that still rings true today.

The blatant refusal to promote minorities over their white counterparts became an issue. To add insult to injury: allegedly, there was a traditional witch-hunt every Thanksgiving and Christmas holiday. This high ranking officer would literally terminate minorities with minor blemishes on their records, just for kicks, leaving their families in a depressed state for the holidays. If this is indeed true, which I am sure it was. What a soul-less bastard and karma is a bitch. If you worked on Rikers Island, you knew this to be true.

Under this Mayor's leadership he equipped his appointees with enormous power to institute his Arnold Schwarzenegger crush kill destroy approach. His cohorts condoned and encouraged correction officers to use force and whatever measures necessary to maintain order in the jails.

In addition to, the preceding Mayors failure to supervise brought upon these incidents below. These incidents are just the tip of the iceberg. These dictators definitely think they are above the law. Nothing is a secret behind the prison walls. Everything is common knowledge amongst the correction department personnel. These are insiders knowledge;

*A Warden who had a history of conducting criminal activities from the time he became a correction Officer until he retired. During his tenure as a captain, he was responsible for drugs and 007 weapons in some of the jails. If an inmate wanted illegal favors, he'd ask for money, he would say "what you going to do for me" It's alleged this same Captain, supplied the inmates with guns. The higher ups knew and covered it up. The surprising thing; the media never reported it and I am quite sure they knew. Inmates were jumping over hoops to be transferred to this building, to be near this "what you going to do for me lowlife captain". Oh yes he is a lowlife because his actions placed officers lives in danger. Ask any criminal on the street if they knew of a captain, granting special illegal favors, changing documents and bringing in drugs and weapons. His name will roll easily off their tongues like butter. Well in spite of his corrupt actions, he climbed the ranks and made it all the way to Warden, and has since retired.

*A Rikers Island **Warden** was driving a vehicle and pulled over by the police. Allegedly, he was arrested by the police, for possession of a couple of kilos of cocaine in his car. The entire ordeal was swept under the rug. No criminal charges, no media coverage, no disciplinary action from the correction department, and he was later promoted.

*A Rikers Island **Warden** whose heroin-addicted son was arrested on felony charges. The official court paperwork was doctored to enable his son, the prisoner, could walk out the back door, after he was placed on Department of Correction's property. Incarceration means exactly that.

He is not entitled to special privileges because he is the Warden's son. The Warden committed a crime and should have been thrown in jail.

*The **Assistant Deputy Warden** who would have weekend cocaine parties at his home. Special invited guest Captains Deputy Wardens and Wardens. High-ranking officers were not drug tested. They were all three-time losers, buying, possessing and using. Drug use among ranking officer was at an all time high in the 80's.

*The **Deputy Warden** who worked with female prisoners on Rikers Island would engage in regular rampant sex every night he worked. Night after night this female inmate would be escorted out of her cell, and into his office. Guess what, she got pregnant. Did you ever hear about this? Hell no ! Another cover up, tsk tsk tsk   .

*Allegedly a **Commissioner**, who I would classify as a Pimp, would either visit the Correction Officer training academy or send his flunkies to the academy looking for fresh ripe new recruit female meat to prey on. You know like a pimp visits the bus stop looking for teenage runaways. He lures them to this big fabulous fancy house in the Pocono's that was probably built or at the least modernized with your taxpaying dollars. This is when the prostitution begins. The female recruits sell their souls using drugs and having sex with the Commissioner and his cronies (probably Wardens, Deputy Wardens, Captains, and Officers) so, they do not have to work with the inmates. They get assignments to any facility or office of their choice. The taxpayers are paying them to sit on their tired asses all day in the office, pushing papers, challenging any and everyone because they have the power of the Pimp daddy Commissioner.

This top dog was indulging and engaging in criminal activity on a daily basis. I never heard of any Commissioner conducting himself in such a disgusting unprofessional manner. He was a pompous predator.

*Allegedly, there were exam and an elite group of correction officers was in a separate room with access to all the correct answers to pass the test. These allegations were allegedly unfounded. There are however, running jokes throughout the correction department that certain Captains were given the answers and that is why they are unfit for their Captains position. These same individuals somehow managed to climb the ranks because of their connection to the Mayor's office.

*Rikers warden charged with assault and harassment after 'kinky' affair

February 29, 2012 According to the New York Post, Corrections Officer Tomara Bryan's discrimination suit charges that in around July 2010 – after Bryan's relationship with a married warden named Emmanuel Bailey became known – Bryan was subjected to "verbal and physical abuse. derogatory comments and unjustified disciplinary actions," in addition to being given "dangerous and/or undesired assignments" and "subjected to a bogus 'random' drug test."

She claims she "suffered severe personal injuries" including "emotional distress, pain and suffering, anxiety, depression, fear and other psychological trauma and injury" as a result of this treatment.

The suit comes nearly seven months after Bailey was arrested on assault and harassment charges after Bryan told cops he had beaten her up during their affair. According to a criminal complaint, Bailey allegedly punched Bryan in the face, kicked her in the stomach, punched a hole in the wall of her Brooklyn apartment and threatened to kill her.

Bailey retired under pressure shortly before that arrest. Court records show Bailey pled guilty to disorderly conduct and received a conditional discharge, according to Brooklyn DA's office.

Bailey's career included a controversial decision to allow gangsta rapper Papoose to do a show at Rikers in 2006 that set off months of violence at the jail.

This is just a little taste of how ranking officers behave. This above the law behavior is partly the blame for screwed up prison system. These higher ups are not doing the job they were hired to do, but spending the tax payers check. If they would truly lead with great intentions, the prison system might be improved.

I have worked with some great male and female bosses. I have also worked with many horrible supervisors. There is nothing worse that a boss singling you out and busting your chops every time they see you. I've dealt with a couple of those bad apple bosses, who would try to set me up and ask for written reports for bullshit. I would submit my report along with something incriminating they did. That kept them off my back.

CHAPTER 4

WHAT IS A PRISONER/INMATE?

When a Rikers Island Correction Officer thinks the current leadership in hugging a Rikers Island thug and catering to rapist, murderers, thieves, arsonists, burglars and pedophiles and believes the current leadership is catering to Rikers Island prisoners, and allowing them to dictate policy. We lost the battle. I do not know how many times I will stress throughout the book. When you go to Rikers Island; you have only been accused of a crime. We cannot pick and choose who we play judge and jury to. Ninety-five percent have yet to have their day in court. I know many may not like that statement; but its true. What's crazy is when one of my colleagues is accused of a crime. None of the above applies. Double standard.

As a correction officer, I primarily worked in the trenches around male prisoners, accused of every crime imaginable from the accused rapists to the accused murderers, my entire career. Mind you without a weapon to defend myself. I did not sit in an office position batting my eyes and filing my nails, while on my knee pleasuring a superior like some of my female colleagues; who were afraid of getting their hands dirty? I worked on Rikers Island, the New York City borough jails and court facilities amid male prisoners. Therefore, I think after working with prisoners for twenty years, I am in the best position to give you the 411 on what exactly a prisoner is. They are not as bad as people think.

What is a prisoner? Many people really have no idea. The Webster definition: A prisoner, also known as an inmate or detainee, is a person who is, deprived of liberty against his or her will. This can be by confinement, captivity or by forcible restraint. This term applies particularly to those on trial or serving a prison sentence in a prison.

For many years, the general public had to rely on television shows and the news for prison narratives. Unfortunately, the typical television portrayal and interpretation, is just an inkling of what a prisoner is. They describe prisoners as, the bad guys, thugs, animals, scumbags, lowlife, misfits. The list goes on.

The horrible depiction leads the public to fear and assume these people are locked up for a reason and must have committed a crime, or done something wrong otherwise they would not be in jail. That theory is so incorrect and wrong on so many levels, and the social media antidote for exposing the inaccuracies, is viral media and exposing injustices.

It is my opinion approximately 50% of the prisoners on Rikers Island are innocent. They have not been convicted of a crime only accused, meanwhile we treat them as though they are convicted murderers. even if they are only arrested for minor offense. Society is so brainwashed, the minute someone utters Rikers Island , jail or prison. Our first response is not a pleasant one.

My definition of an inmate is someone who has been accused, falsely accused, convicted or tricked into admitting to a crime, that they did not do, or just plain ole guilty. Many are very smart people that either have done something dumb and were caught or did absolutely nothing wrong and karma is a bitch.

Some people presume they know what an inmate, prisoner or convict is, and really do not understand how unfair the judicial system is and as Americans we are jaded by what we hear or see on TV. If you have never been arrested or seen the inside of a prison, this is foreign territory that you will never understand. It is my goal to enlightened you and make you have a better understanding. I am tired of people turning their noses up to incarcerated people.

The entire judicial system is one big racket. People's lives are bartered from the very beginning, sometimes before the arrest.

Quotas have to be made, in order for law officials to stay in the limelight of their cushiony positions. There are times when a police officer will arrest someone they know is innocent, just to reach that quota for the day.

The person arrested does not have any money so they are at the mercy of the courts and appointed a legal aid attorney to represent them. The legal aid in turn negotiates with the district attorney. If the prisoner will not accept the terms and conditions, because they know, they are innocent. Nine times out of ten, they will sit in jail for up to three years going back and forth to court, due to the backlog. They call it bullpen therapy.

The district attorney does not want to set the person free even though they know they are innocent and have absolutely no evidence, because the courts will have to pay that individual for everyday they were wrongfully incarcerated, and that does not look good on the prosecutor's record. Therefore, a person can sit on Rikers Island for years and be completely innocent and are ostracized by the courts, because the prosecutor does not want to admit they made a mistake.

It's been proven by overturned sentences and an up rise in wrongful convictions with overzealous prosecutors and their crony Judges looking to gain notoriety with a winning conviction records.

Prosecutors do not care if the sentences are overturned because they know it will be almost impossible or can take many years to overturn. The prosecutors thirst for the conviction equals a notch on their belts in a political world.

The sacrificial lamb is the prisoner who is actual a victim of the judicial system. They claim their innocence and spend centuries in jail praying someone helps to prove their innocence, for some it may never happen, because you need thousands of dollars for the proper appeal attorney to have a shot at getting your sentence overturned.

There are some prisoners who will not settle for injustice. They will fight to the very end even if it kills them emotionally and spiritually. They know they are innocent and are being punished because they refuse to succumb to the judicial tactics.

Case and point: Kalief Browder was incarcerated for 3 years while they jerked him around. They figured if they kept him in longer he would be give up his pleas of innocence, just to come home. God bless the dead, but kudos to Kalief because he did not fall for the judicial trickery. He sat in jail innocent for three years and was abuse physically, mentally, emotionally and spiritually. He was a lot stronger than he gave himself credit for. The scars were too deep and he was just a baby with high hopes when he entered the system. He was a target for the judicial system ole playbook of just get the conviction.

I know this to be true because I worked in the attorney visit area in Brooklyn Courts. I met a lot of great legal aide attorney's while working in Brooklyn Courts, who took their jobs seriously and made the difference.

My job description allowed me to deal directly with attorneys, legal aids, 18b's and private attorneys. There are good ones and bad ones. The private and 18b came across as a little more concerned and willing to fight for their clients.

Legal aid attorneys are overworked, underpaid and at times at the mercy of the courts too. Several of the legal aid attorneys appeared stressed and lackadaisical. It is my opinion some of those legal aid attorneys worked directly with the prosecutor and bartered the prisoners life away, like slave trade. Their sentiments "I'll give you this one, you let this one walk," The prosecutor wins his case and the legal aid gets rid of one of hundreds of cases.

I came to this conclusion because some were visually agitated, had a hand full of folders and their conversation would go something like this, "You should take a plea because if you go to trial and will most likely blow trial. You will get 15 yrs to life".

The prisoner's response might be "Get the fuck outta here, I ain't do nothing". or 'This is my first arrest", "I want a new attorney". Often they try to attack them through the metal partition separating them; or just say " Ok, I'll take a plea".

That unnerved me especially since one particular incident the 16 year old adolescent agreed to the 7 years in prison for attempted robbery, with no parents or guardians present. This lawyer probably could have gotten probation, community service or one to three years, especially since it was his first offense. The adolescent said he did not commit the crime. I do not know if that is true or not. He lacked education and had no clue of his rights; What I do know is his life will be ruined, by the time he completes 7 years in prison. He will transition from an adolescent jail to an adult jail when he turns 18. He will have a felony record and will most likely have difficulty surviving in society. Not counting the mental and physical abuse, he will suffer at the hands of correction officers and inmates, by the time he is released. He will be forever violently scarred and broken in more ways than one and take those broken angry scars back to the communities.

By the time you finish reading this chapter, I hope you give you a clearer picture of whom and what a prisoner/inmate is and why the New York jails are destined to become a war zone in the coming years.

For many years, we have been brainwashed into believing everyone in jail is guilty. I spent 20 years in the prison system, from Rikers Island – Brooklyn Court Facilities.

I said it when I became a Correction Officer and I will say it again I do not believe everyone in jail is guilty or deserves imprisonment.

Prisons are a racket and, have become big business for the corporate giants, and each prisoner represents financial gain. Businesses make money to feed, bathe and cloth inmates. I believe contracts are given to businesses that are connected to some official somewhere in these law departments.

Just think about it, where are they getting their food, toilet paper, soap and clothing supplies .

In order for a business to thrive, you need customers. If no one is in jail or the population is low; prison contracts are cut and people are out of jobs.

The primary targets are the underprivileged and disadvantaged and its pure racial. No, I am not a militant pulling the race card: I'm a realist. All you have to do is look at the overall jail populations in New York.

Minorities are the most deprived. All the necessary tools to make their communities thrive and survive have diminished throughout the years.

What troubles me the most is people from the brighter walk of life, are biased and want to blame the minorities and communities until it happens to them or their family members.

One of my primary reason for compassion I have for some prisoners in this book is: To a certain degree, looking back now, it is because of them, I was able to retire. On many occasions; they were my backup when my colleagues would voluntarily disappear, leaving me alone to fend for myself with hundreds of male prisoners at a time.

Some of my colleagues were unprofessional and placed my life in a dangerous position, whether it was unintentional or intentionally. (I believe the latter on many instances)

I recall working on the midnight tour, alone behind a locked steel gate, in the back of the dorm areas, with close to 200 male prisoners to watch.

My colleague who was supposed to be watching my back was in a comatose state in the front officer's station.

I guess if they wanted to rape, kill or beat the living hell out of me, they had plenty of time because obviously my co-worker came to work to sleep and not watch the prisoners or my back. Nevertheless, my opinion varies from inmate to inmate.

They have a saying among correction officers that an inmate is an inmate not your friend. What I say to that is an inmate is not your friend, but he is not your enemy either. Trust me, they had easy access to take me hostage.

I look at our old NYC Correction Commissioner Bernard Kerik. You know the one who went to jail. I wonder how many people looked at him the same way they looked at any average minority inmate that is sentenced to prison time. I wonder if he was starved ,chained, shackled, physically abused and tortured. How many beat downs did he endure because he made eye contact with a correction officer.? Was he beat down, threatened and told he better refuse medical attention ?

How many correction ranking officers still considered ex Commissioner Bernard Kerik their friend while he was serving his prison term?

You are more likely to be stabbed in the back by a colleague before an inmate. I learned early to be less judgmental, and realize inmates are regular people, and by the grace of God, I was never in that situation.

Looking back now, my overall assessment of what an inmate represents is that of a slave in a plantation. Regardless to how they got there, they lost their freedom and have to dance to someone else's music, desperately want to go home, their masters feed them when and what they feel like feeding them, hate them and want to punish them. They're starved, chained, shackled, physically abused and tortured on many occasions for doing absolutely nothing, just breathing.

CHAPTER 5

YOUR FIRST TIME IN PRISON

If you have never been to prison, you have no idea what to expect or what you are up against. I have seen many first timers terrified and in shock. They figure they do not belong there and many of the prisoners do. Therefore, they turn their noses up, sit as far away as possible from the other prisoners because they do not want to give the wrong impression. Guess what, you are just like everyone in jail and the other prisoners will resent your high-cidity-ness and teach you a jail lesson you will never forget.

You will probably be beaten and robbed by the other prisoners, while the officers ignore your pleas for help. They too shun people who think they are better than anyone else. Yes its your first time and you feel like you do not belong there. However you better assess, adjust and adapt to your surroundings or you are creating a toxic environment for your well being.

I remember in the 60's when I was a little girl and the police came to my house and arrested my father.

Let me tell you. My father is one of the nicest, most honest people you could ever encounter. He is a good guy and was working two jobs, a conductor for New York City Transit and a dental technician; and literally will not hurt a fly. He was accused assaulting someone he did not know.

Yes, he went through the prison system, yes he had never been arrested and, yes probably had that attitude that he did not belong there.

When the Correction Officers began to search him and wanted him to drop his pants and bend over, squat and cough. He thought they were out of their minds and refused. Well, the correction officers beat him up. I just found that out when I started writing this book. The charges were eventually dropped but at 76 years old, he still remembers this traumatic experience.

Therefore, I know first hand anyone can go to jail and, everyone is a potential prisoner including you, and yes, including me. You do not have to do anything wrong. I know I am not exempt. Yes, this retired New York City Correction Officer, revealing all the dirty dark secrets and what really goes on inside the city and state jails is now a target and I could care less. The truth is what matters to me, and the public has a right to know.

This chapter is important because the average person, who plays by the rules, does everything right, does not bother anyone, lives a clean drama free life, can wind up behind bars, in a blink of an eye. I know you are reading the title of this chapter and thinking there is no way you are going to jail. You will never be a prisoner. You do not commit crimes, not a criminal or hang out with undesirables. Therefore, you could never go to jail. You are ready to skip to the next chapter. That is where you are dead wrong and need to pay close attention. I will take you systematically into what your fate will look like. if you or your family member are arrested.

*Remember** that ticket you got for running a red light. You know the moving violation ticket the cop gave you, that's, sitting in your pocket book. You know the one they keep sending you from the parking violation bureau and you were adamant you were not going to pay. Guess what? Your license has probably been suspended because you were too stubborn or lazy to pay the ticket. Now, the police just pulled you over for that broken tail light, or an illegal u turn you just took. Well sweetie pie, you are going to jail.

Yes, this might be minor, but you will spend at least 2-3 days with Correction Officers and prisoners. Everybody goes through the jail system and to let the courts figure it out.

You will go from central booking to the court bullpens. Bullpens is slang for the large cells they cram every prisoners into. Guess who runs the bullpens in New York City. My wonderful, darling colleagues, the Correction Officers from the New York City Department of Correction". Yes, you will be under the "Care, custody and control "of Correction Officers. Depending upon which one of my colleagues that are working, during each shift will determine what type of demeanor and treatment you get. Whatever you do, do not get on their bad side because they will tamper with your paperwork and it will take forever for you to go in front of a judge.

The bullpens to the courts are normally filled to capacity with inmates who have been sitting there for anywhere from 24 to 72 hours. The bullpen is large, has one toilet and stinks to high heaven. If someone happens to take a dump, everyone smells it, including the correction officers. Now you will sit there and wait anywhere from 24-72 hours for the Correction Officer to call out your name.

At that point, a police officer will escort you to the courtroom and you will appear in front of a judge to plead your case. If you do not have an attorney, one will be appointed to you prior to your appearance. You will appear in front of the judge and if they do not let you go home. You will be escorted back to the bullpen and off to Rikers Island you go. This is where some of the Correction Officers will consider you guilty even though you have only been accused.

Oh remember what mama always told you. "Always leave the house with clean underwear". If you are arrested and have to go to Rikers Island, expect to strip down butt naked, bend down, cough, spread your butt cheeks and lift your balls and breast. Expect that every time you go on a visit or have to leave the building. No its not the doctor's office. It's jail and you will be visually examined to make sure you have no weapons' on you.

There is a thin line between freedom on the streets and incarceration. No one is exempt. Ask Bernard Kerik, Sheldon Silver and Martha Stewart etc,.

We now live in a vicious vindictive world and at any given moment someone can lie on you and you will land in jail and it will be up to the judge and jury to decide your fate.

I will give you a couple of scenarios to show you how easy it is to be arrested.

*You meet up with one of your friends or an associate. While driving your car, you get pulled over by the police. What you did not know, is your friend had drugs in their possession and threw it on your car floor. Your passenger is not going to cop to the ownership because they do not want to go to jail. It is your car and you will take the weight. Hello! You are now a prisoner!

*A man (CEO of a big company) and a woman (a nurse) are in a relationship. The man is cheating on his wife and she finds out, and the man files for divorce. The wife injures herself and files a false report that the husband assaulted her. The CEO is now a prisoner sitting in jail; maybe temporary or for a period of time, because the his wife lied.

*Your adult daughter is in an abusive relationship. Her husband beat her the crap out of her and she is in intensive care. You round up the boys and decide to teach him a lesson. You beat him to a pulp. Hello jail cell !

*Your child comes home with a black eye from the bully kid down the block. You confront the parent and a fight ensues. Hello jail cell !

*You child decides they no longer want to listen to you and breaks all the rules. You decide go upside their heads and your darling child calls the police, or tell the teacher in school that you beat them, trying to get sympathy, and the teacher contacts the authorities

*A guy is in a long term relationship with a female. They have children together. They break up and the woman is devastated. The guy moves on and gets a new girlfriend. The ex is angry and wants revenge. She accuses him of sexual molesting their little daughter.

48

At any given moment, something so small can transpire in your life and that situation can land you in jail. You do not necessarily have to do anything. Just think about it. How many times has someone lied on you at work to get your position? On the other hand, accused you of something you did not do. No, it is not jail worthy but no one believed you. The judicial welcoming party does greet you with balloons and a cake, after an allegation has been made.

You have now become what society believes is the scum of the earth. The word inmate has been overrated, stigmatized and deemed dirty. Almost like the Ebola virus and any other situation that people do not understand. If you catch Ebola you can possible die, if you are not cured of it. If you get arrested and go to jail you can possibly do hard time or die. Look at the inmates in Riker's Island that died.

You can do everything right in life, follow all the rules and a weird scenario may occur and you are arrested. You are supposed to be innocent until proven guilty. That is total bullshit. Today's court system is you are guilty until proven innocent. At that point, you will most likely enter the Rikers Island hell hole and guess what you are now an inmate and that stench is attached to your name, even if you win the case.

Are you a scum bag thug? No! Nevertheless you are innocent? Right? It does not matter, you have been incarcerated and the world looks at you differently. You will sit on Rikers Island month after month, while they continuously adjourn your case, until you are fed up and plead guilty to get it over with, even though they are innocent, now they have a criminal record. That will follow you for the rest of your life. It is difficult to get a job and your life is in more shambles that you could imagine. So please pay attention to this book , because your life may depend on it.

CHAPTER 6

RIKERS "HELLS" ISLAND

I worked on Rikers Island for a short period in my career and I can tell you its worst than people could possibly imagine. It was horrible unclean and depressing.

I started working on Rikers Island in May 1983 in New York City Correctional Institution for Men. I was 21 years old, enthusiastic and in high spirits. I had a good paying job in law enforcement and enjoyed going to work.

Working in an all male prison was a walk in the park; literally. I grew up in the Brownsville housing projects, so for me, it was like walking down Stone Avenue. I recognized many faces and was never afraid to walk within the realm of incarcerated men.

The high spirits and enthusiasm began to diffuse. I never imagined I would be subjected to verbal, physical and emotional abuse by my colleagues. In less than two years, I would be assaulted by one of my male colleagues, treated like shit by some of my female colleagues, targeted like a runway at a bus stop, and ran off Rikers Island by a womanizing Warden.

Contrary to what people think I did not want to leave Rikers Island because I met my future husband, Correction Officer Ronnie Purvis.

However I didn't have a choice because Warden "Hollywood" Bains, was going after my job. I don't think he appreciated my response, when he approached my work area (annex lower gate) and snapped his finger and pointed for me to unlock the steel gate, to enable him to walk through.

That prompted me to laugh in his face hysterically. Yes it was unprofessional, but I am not fido, and snapping your fingers and pointing for me to open a gate was not the proper way an officer should be instructed, by a superior officer; case closed.

Obviously the Warden didn't appreciate my reluctance to bow down like some of my female and male colleagues, who feared him; so he begin gunning for me. I knew had I not transferred out, I would have been set up and fired.

I cannot say that is the best thing that happened to me because as I soon learned, no matter where you go, the Rikers Island mentality exists everywhere in the New York City prison facilities, within the correction officer's mindset.

I have not worked there in years, but judging from what I am reading in the newspapers and the people I encounter in the streets that either work there or have family members that work there, it's the same reminiscences. The only difference is the media is finally all on it now.

Therefore, what exactly is the Rikers Island everybody keeps ranting about? If you never been on the Rikers Island, it sits in the East River, (not literally) between Queens and the mainland Bronx adjacent to the runways of LaGuardia Airports. You could never imagine what goes on in Rikers Island.

This is a Yelp review:" Great vacation getaway if you like getting your butt kicked by both inmates and officers. Food is decent but I've had a lot better from the dollar menu. Floors are dirty. I have seen bedbugs crawling around the size of roaches. Gotta wash your underwear in the sink if your unlucky you will have to do them for others" Kind of funny but not really, because its true.

Most people just say "THE ROCK" or "THE ISLAND." I call it that land of testosterone. It is a male dominated atmosphere, where egos are not, left at the door. In fact, correction officer's egos are encouraged to enter. You hear all these stories about going to Rikers Island or you may have visited it and vowed to never return, because the CO's were very loud, boisterous, abusive and disrespectful. There have been many complaints from lawyers and family members, regarding the mistreatment they received from the guards. They felt they were treated you as though they were criminals.

The media reporting continuous correction officers misconduct: drugs sales, abusive tactics, murder, rapes and sex with inmates, has changed people's opinions about Rikers Island and some are egging on closure. I think that is ludicrous because where will you house the existent bad guys. There are still some horrible criminals roaming the streets and prisons. In addition to many Correction Officers are the problem. You close Rikers Island and the same officers are still in charge.

Rikers Island has approximately 10 jails. In order to get into the jails you have to cross this long bridge, we call it the Rikers Island Bridge. When you first get on the bridge, you can see the end of the bridge. It looks like a big creepy mouth with fire spitting. Indicative of a hell-hole, and the devil's haven.

Rikers "Hell's" Island is what I call it, and many would agree. Reason being: it is not a place you want to live or visit. It is a person's worst nightmare, a negative mean environment, and you may not make it out alive. Your civil rights will more likely than not be violated on a regular basis. As a prisoner, it is dreadful enough you have to worry about your safety regarding your fellow prisoner. If a Correction Officer takes a disliking to you, they can make your life a living hell and can turn the inmates against you. That too has been recently reported in the media.

A large percentage of the Correction Officers hate the job; but love the paycheck and power that comes along with. If you make it out alive and in one piece, trust me, you will be forever mentally and emotionally scarred .

Once you get across that long Rikers Island Bridge, you are introduced to one main building. That main building is the central nervous system, where all the searching of your body parts begins. They have now extended that pleasure of walking through the metal detector to my colleagues. With all the drugs entering the jails, they now know, the correction officers are partly to blame too.

Correction Officers are presently being subjected to, almost, the same type of degrading search, they have subjected a visitor to. Eventually they will search correction officers as they do prisoners that enter Rikers Island, remove your underwear, bend down, squat and cough. This in itself is very sad.

Rikers Island has numerous buildings once you leave the main building. These buildings are where the prisoners are housed .

As a Correction Officer you have no idea what lies ahead in one of those inmate filled buildings, as that gate slams shut behind you, when you about to assume the visual role of a Correction Officer for that day.

You have to watch out for the inmates who can be very dangerous, but you, kind of, knew that already, when you graduated out of the correction-training academy. As a Correction Officer, you would never think that you would have to watch out for your colleagues, who could be so unprofessional, nasty, vicious and vindictive towards you.

Nevertheless, some of you know this because you have visited Rikers or know a correction officer, and experienced this vicious behavior. If you knew, a Correction Officer before they became a guard at Rikers Island. You have actually witnessed the horrible transformation.

Once inside Rikers Island, some Correction Officers transform into this dark creature, out of necessity. Jail is dark and no matter how much you brighten the day, and look on the brighter side of life, it is a negative environment. You are dealing with a bunch of people who lost their freedom.

Rikers Island is indicative of a large plantation. Oh, please do not be shocked I wrote that. I am about to go deep, real deep and when I break it down to you, maybe you will get it, maybe you will not. This is not a militant racial thing, its reality. So I am going to keep it real. No candy-coating in this book.

When a person loses their freedom to the judicial system, they become a slave to whomever is in charge of them. Why do I use the term slave? They tell you when and how you move and it is a big adjustment for grown ass men and women, white, black, brown or green. Not so much for kids, because they are still somewhat under the supervision of their parents. Rikers Island does not discriminate.

I spent 20 years as a Correction Officer and seen a lot. NYCDOC is a messy organization. At this point I could care less which one of my colleagues is offended or will be offended by what I am about to write in this chapter. It is the truth and people need to be educated because they could end up in this hellhole.

So looking back now, analyzing and assessing my 1983-2005 career in this big giant correction organization. It reminds me of a modern day slavery and at present, I feel like I sold my soul to the devil for a paycheck.

Correction personnel and inmates become slaves in some form or fashion, whether they realize it or not, especially Correction Officers. Oh and it does not matter what rank or color you were.

In the 1980's the roster of the slave chain of command was as follows. Correction Officer, Captain, Assistant Deputy Warden, Deputy Warden, Warden, Chief of Operations and Commissioner. They have since changed the titles with Division Chiefs. My interpretation in the 1980's were as follows: The plantation owner Mayor and Commissioner, the house niggas, and the field niggas. If the Mayor is not directly giving the orders, the Commissioners definitely have a hand in molding the bullshit.

Next, it is the house niggas and field niggas. The field niggas are the inmates of course, some of the correction officers, captains and ranking officers too. Oh and at that point, it does not matter what color you are. The "field niggas" are the least respected.

The correction officers who are field niggas, are looked upon as, undesirable misfits of the department. They do not fit in with the agenda of the house niggas for whatever reason. They are considered rejects, and treated with, little to no respect. They normally try to do everything in their power to be, accepted, by the house niggas.

HOUSE NIGGAS:

The house niggas are the ones with connections to the plantation owners, directly or indirectly. They carry out orders of their plantation owners and abuse the power they have over the field niggas . They are protected by their house nigga peers and or the slave owners. They can be found, in cliques, throughout the department and some inmates are part of this clique because they are either kin, drug dealer or hit man to a correction employee.

FIELD NIGGAS: INMATES

The field niggas were the inmates of course and some of the Correction Officers, Captains and ranking officers. As I have stated, the inmate field niggas are the least respected. They are looked, upon as the scum of the earth. Many Rikers Island employees have already played judge, jury and executioner: they have already been presumed guilty, even if it this their first time in jail, or they've been wrongfully convicted.

FIELD NIGGAS:

CORRECTION AND RANKING OFFICERS

The Correction Officers and Ranking officer (field niggas) (remember it does not matter what skin color you are) are the misfits. They do not fit in with the agenda of the house niggas for whatever reason. They too, are shunned upon, and treated with, less respect.

Are you following me thus far? I know this can be quite confusing.

Rikers Island is basically, filled with a bunch of cliques (mini gangs). If you do not belong to any cliques they will make your life a living hell.

PLANTATION OWNERS:

COMMISSIONERS AND MAYORS

The plantation owners are the Commissioners and Mayors. They're overseers by New York City Department of Correction. Depending upon who has the power of those positions, will most likely determine the **mindset** of the house niggas and determine the fate of the field niggas.

This breakdown reflects my opinion during my tenure as a Correction Officer.

Nevertheless, the slave/plantation owners from the 80's -2005 some of who should have been thrown in the fire

The textbook version of Rikers Island today is as follows.

The jail complex, operated by the New York City Department of Correction, has a budget of $860 million a year, a staff of 9,000 officers and 1,500 civilians managing 100,000 admissions per year and an average daily population of 14,000 inmates.

The Rikers Island complex, which consists of ten jails, holds local offenders who are awaiting trial and cannot afford, obtain, or were not given bail from a judge, those serving sentences of one year or less and those temporarily placed there pending transfer to another facility. Rikers Island is therefore a jail and not a prison, which typically holds offenders serving longer-term sentences. It is home to ten of the New York City Department of Corrections' fifteen facilities and can accommodate up to 15,000 prisoners.

Facilities located on the island include Otis Bantum Correctional Center (OBCC), Robert N. Davoren Complex (RNDC, formerly ARDC), Anna M. Kross Center (AMKC), George Motchan Detention Center (GMDC), North Infirmary Command (NIC), Rose M. Singer Center (RMSC), Eric M. Taylor Center (EMTC, formerly CIFM), James A. Thomas Center (JATC) (no longer used to house inmates),[8] George R. Vierno Center (GRVC) and West Facility (WF). The Bantum, Kross, Motchan, and Vierno house detained male adults. Eric M Taylor houses sentenced male adolescents and adults. Davoren primarily houses male inmates who are of ages 16 through 18. Rose M. Singer houses detained and sentenced female adolescents and adults. North Infirmary primarily houses inmates who require medical attention from an infirmary. West Facility houses inmates who have diseases that are contagious. The average daily inmate population on the island is about 14,000, although it can hold a maximum of 15,000. The daytime population (including staff) can be 20,000 or more

However, it is notorious for abuse and neglect of prisoners in recent years, which has attracted increased media and judicial scrutiny that resulted in numerous rulings against the New York City government. In May 2013, Rikers Island ranked as one of the ten worst prisons in the

United States, based on reporting in Mother Jones magazine.

Rikers Island has recently been the subject of press and judicial action after numerous incidents of abuse and neglect of prisoners; in 2013, there were 129 instances of physical injury inflicted by guards, including punctured organs and broken bones.

The Rikers Island in the early 1980's was a mini version of what is going on today.

The correctional corruption you read about today on Rikers Island, is nothing new and has been going on for many years. Crossing that fine line is so easy to the weak .

CHAPTER 7

"I CAN'T BREATHE"
SOLITARY CONFINMENT

Solitary Confinement and gang-style beatings by Correction Officers, go hand in hand. It is my opinion that large amount of inmates are in Solitary Confinement today because they were lied on or set-up by a Correction Officer. Yes many are there for inmate fights and stabbings that could have been prevented if the correction officers paid attention. In jail an inmate may be faced with a kill or be killed situation. As a prisoner, which would you prefer.

Solitary confinement is the worst form of torture any human being can endure in prison. I would not wish that on my worst enemy. To be thrown in a dark cell , with cement walls and a thick metal door, that slams shut behind you That can literally drive a person insane. Prison is confining enough. Solitary confinement is a prison within a prison. You could never truly understand how it feels, unless you are in that type of confinement, day in day out. Its horrific and degrading. To a certain degree Correction Officers are subjected to low level solitary confinement.

Now, I want you to imagine yourself alone in an old office building, on the fifteenth floor working at your desk. It is a cold winter night, and you decided to stay late in the office to catch up on your work. You lost track of time, you pack up and rush to the elevator. You always hated this elevator because it is small, dirty, cold and creepy.

You get on the elevator, press the button, and watch as the arrow points downward each level. All of a sudden, the elevator comes to a complete halt and it is now pitch black. You stand there for a minute to collect your thoughts and realized it is Friday evening, midnight to be exact, and the building closed early for an extended holiday weekend.

The maintenance man must have thought everyone left the building and shut the power off. You reach for your cell phone and realize you have no reception. You use the light from the cell phone as a guide to the elevator panel and begin pressing the buttons and yelling, "I'm in here, hello "hoping someone will hear you. Several minutes have passed and your voice is now hoarse from screaming.

You are in panic mode because you realize you will have to sit there until Tuesday because Monday is a holiday. Eventually you fall asleep, after crying for several two hours.

I want you to briefly close your eyes for about two minutes, and place yourself in that elevator. (close your eyes)

You wake up several hours later and realize it is now six o'clock Saturday and reality sits in. You have no food or water. There is only one bar left on your phone and you cannot make a call. There goes your light. You feel dirty sitting in the nasty elevator and cannot take a shower. At this point, you begin to freak out.

Imagine what your mindset will be on Tuesday morning after sitting in this casket type setting for several days. Welcome to New York City and State Correctional solitary confinement.

This is the worse form of torture any human being should have to endure. The only difference between being stuck in an elevator for a couple of days, and solitary confinement in a prison, is the elevator scenario, you will be able to leave in about a day or two and go on with your normal life. In prison, your stay in that catastrophic environment significantly longer.

Residing in prison is horrifying enough for a detainee or sentenced prisoner. It takes a toll on your psyche, more so, when wrongfully detained, wrongfully convicted or wrongfully placed in solitary confinement because Correction Officers lied on you or planted a weapon in your cell. .

If you are lucky, you will not experience a Guantanamo Bay like solitary confinement equipped with water boarding, gang style beating or any form of torture by Correction Officer.

Ask the inmates from Clinton Correctional Facility, who stated they had no knowledge of the prison break and allegedly received the Guantanamo bay special from the correction officers there, with the alleged blessings of the administration.

I want to reach out to all celebrities, Jay Z's, Bill Gates, Bill Cosby, Bill Clinton, Rand Paul, Dick Cheney, politicians and any high profile person. Solitary confinement is where you will end up, if you are falsely accused or accused of a crime. It is protective custody aka solitary confinement. You may have bail money and bail out after a couple of days. However, while awaiting the process, you will be in solitary confinement isolated from everyone else, because you will be considered a high profile prisoner.

If you are lucky to bail out and stupid enough to violate the terms of the release like ex-Commissioner Bernard Kerik did. Solitary confinement will be your home while the courts decide your fate.

Solitary Confinement ;often referred to as the box, the hole, protective custody, punitive segregation, administrative and segregation, dungeon, torture chamber, cracker tunnel in a prison facility.

In actually the entire New York State maximum-security jails are reminiscent of a solitary confinement type setting. The New York State inmates, in a maximum-security prison, only leave their cells briefly. They will most likely spend anywhere from 18-23 hours a day in their cells.

Through my eyes and knowledge, you will understand what solitary confinement is and how it affects people, and why it needs to end. I will also offer a solution and alternative to ending this Guantanamo Bay type punishment instituted in the prison system. The state is ignoring and denying. Whoever, came up with this theory to place inmates in solitary confinement, obviously has never actually sat in one. The entire criminal justice system and federal government lack compassion, until it happens to one of their own. They know this systematic act of cruelty is inhumane and they simply do not care

I want you to keep in mind the Rikers Island population is primarily prisoners who are only "accused" of a crime, "not convicted "of a crime.

Not to be contradictory, nevertheless, there are some instances whereas, I think there are some dangerous monsters are in jail and need some type of isolation.

If an inmate is extremely dangerous to himself or others, he should be isolated. At that point, he should cross over to the mental health division section.

I have a problem with the process of determining which inmates are transferred to punitive (disciplinary) solitary confinement; in particular, the cases whereas correction officers are making false allegations following gang style beatings and the failure of the inmate to physically defend themselves. In other words they are being jumped by correction officers and do not fight back.

During the hearing, it is their word against the Correction Officers word. Correction Officers using excessive force citing bogus "assault on officer" charges will always win a case. The superior officer from that institution will most likely conduct the hearing, and will more likely than not, base their final decision in favor of the correction officer's, accounts of what transpired.

Why? The inmate will have grounds to sue, and if successful, that will cost the taxpayers a lot of money. As well as the superior officer who was on duty at the time of the incident. They might be penalized, for failure to supervise. They are more interested in climbing the ranks and a failure to supervise will tarnish their record. Therefore, I would say 90% of the hearings are rigged. In fact the state inspector general told my nephew, who was beat down by New York State Correction Officers, he would lose his hearing, even though he had eyewitness testimony (correction officer and 50 inmates).

*(see chapter on " Greenhaven Correctional Facility")

Therefore, if you do not accept as true, I challenge the Albany and the city and state Attorney General to investigate the main punitive segregation buildings, on Rikers Island "OBCC" and New York State "Southport Correctional Facility".

Open all records to "assault on correction officers". Look to see; how many inmates allegedly assaulted correction officers? How many Correction Officer hospitalized? (Not visited a hospital emergency room to cover their asses) You could probably count it on one hand. How many inmates prosecuted for assaulting an officer? You will find one to every one hundred, might have assaulted a correction officer. The rest received gang style beatings by the guards.

I am familiar with this playbook firsthand because I watched the cover-ups as a New York City Correction Officer. I saw the playbook being utilized by New York State Correction Officers. My nephew spent one year in NYS Southport Correctional Facility in solitary confinement. I witness first hand how correction and superior officer's cover-up a gang style beating.

New York State Department of Corrections has a full blown out motive for solitary confinement. Big Business! (That's right money talks, bullshit walks.)

In order for there to be solitary confinement in jails, you need clients. I refer to them as victims in most cases. These solitary confinement sections and designated buildings in state corrections have to remain open for the purpose of continued big business.

Therefore, when the population diminishes in Southport Correctional Facility , I would assume someone picks up the phone and tells them the count is low, get the goon squad, we need more clients, and some inmates become targets. You cannot justify a budget for an empty solitary confinement. Each body equals dollars. It is my opinion this happens more than likely in a state prison facility vs. a city jail.

Rikers Island became the focus of inhumane solitary confinement practices with housing adolescents prisoners. What do they do? Their solution to reforming solitary confinement was to institute a bogus new policy called, Enhanced Supervision Unit (ESHU) You can put lipstick on a pig and it is still a pig.

When you are placed into solitary confinement: You will not receive phone calls, programs, no group interaction with other inmates and out of cell movement except an hour a day of legally mandated recreation.

If you decide to go to recreation, you will be "mechanically restrained" with handcuffs and a waist chain as you are escorted to an empty outdoor cage. If you have a history of violence, you will remain shackled during recreation. If the temperature outside is below freezing, you will not be allowed to wear gloves or a hat. There is no equipment in the recreation cell, not even a ball.

At dinnertime, a rubber-gloved hand pushes a meal tray through the feed slot in your door. You cannot see the face of the person serving your food. As evening turns to night, you lie down to sleep but cannot. The shouts of men in neighboring cells ricochet down the corridors and bounce off the concrete walls, creating an eerie hullabaloo. From the wild ranting of a particular inmate, you can tell that he has lost his mind. Hours later, you wonder what time it is but have no way of knowing since watches are not allowed and no clocks are in sight. The newspaper the correction officer gives you the next day is a week old. Your only contact with the outside world is through a single earphone you plug into a wall jack connecting you to a few radio stations chosen by the facility. It occurs to you how little control you have left over your world: You cannot choose what you hear, what you read, what you see. Your surroundings have been reduced to shadows and steel, your life to a nightmarish monotony.

What this sounds like to me is a plantation within a prison. Why do I say that? You know why, every jail is highly populated with minorities. It makes me wonder if the prison system would be different, if everything switched gears and the jail population suddenly became majority white, would the rules change or would they just target only the minorities and cater to the white inmates, as they do now. They put so much trust in white prisoners, they are literally walking out the door.

The correction department exhibits abuse of power using solitary confinement to abuse and violate the civil rights of many inmates.

Solitary confinement is constantly hanging over inmates head while in prison. Like in the slavery days, "If you don't do this john boy the master is going to be upset and put you in the hole ". If you rub the master the wrong way john boy, the master is going to put you in the hole ". " Don't look the master in the eyes john boy, or he is going to put you in the hole, Stay away from the master today john boy, he looks upset, and is going to put you in the hole "

The bottom line is a large majority of correction and ranking officers take the control part of "care custody and control "to another level. It is too much power for a correction officer to have over an inmate, when it comes to the determination of their freedom, within the jail system.

Let me give you an example. How many of you start working at a new job and your boss or someone with influence does not like you. It is nothing you have done or said. They simply do not like you. They go out of their way to make your life a living hell and try to get you fired or transferred.

Well if you are an inmate and a Correction Officer does not like you, your personality or skin color. They know the worst thing you can do to an inmate is place them in solitary confinement.

It is bad enough that inmate could be in jail for something they did not do. Now you want to make their lives more of a living hell by making sure they end up in what I call the coffin cell "solitary confinement" These inmates are at the mercy of correction officers' everyday all day. I want to ask all Correction Officers if they can survive solitary confinement. I seriously doubt it.

Our history making Ex-Commissioner Bernard Kerik wrote about the mental torture of solitary confinement. He was in protective custody his entire stint. If you do not believe me, ask Bernie or Google him! He has flip-flopped on this issue.

He knows exactly how it feels. Ask him is it a human thing to do. He had to endure it all.

I googled him and found this piece of journalism on the internet. Below is Bernard Keriks lawyer's argument to the courts.

"The Government is also opposing Bernie's request for a voluntary surrender. That strikes me as mean-spirited. Most white-collar offenders are allowed to voluntarily surrender to avoid sitting in a county jail for a month while BOP decides where they are going to be placed. In Bernie's case, because of his law enforcement background, he will end up in segregation. That is just punitive and unnecessary, considering he's not a flight risk. He's been home with his wife and family since the Judge revoked and then reinstated his bail last fall, without any violations.

Why can't the Government be satisfied with a just sentence rather than have to go for the extra pound of flesh to make the sentence as miserable as possible for the defendant? "

That was an excerpt I took off the internet. Bernard Kerik's lawyer was arguing that putting his felon client into solitary confinement was a waste of the taxpayers' money. .

White collar, blue collar, black collar, green collar crimes. What is the difference? A crime is a crime. It is good enough for other criminals, but I guess you are a different type of criminal. Bernie, Bernie Bernie; didn't you allegedly have something to do with, or take credit for this new Rikers Island solitary confinement implementing thingy.

It is my opinion that a requirement prior to working in any jail or having the power to make any solitary confinement decisions, from new recruits, all the way to the Mayor's office. It should be mandated they complete a two-hour stint in solitary confinement and I would like to see who handles it and who quits. .

I am not a doctor however I have spent 20 years in the prison system. Claustrophobia is a dangerous condition and anxiety and panic attacks overall can cause mental conditions.

What is the difference between the electric chair and solitary confinement? It is my opinion there is no difference. Death can be the sentence. The government placing innocent inmates in solitary confinement and death row is similar. You cut off circulation and mental stimulation to the brain. Electric chair someone pulls the trigger. Solitary confinement an inmate can pull his own trigger.

A prisoner does not exit solitary confinement better and whole. They exit weak, angry , violent and broken Humans are supposed to have contact with each other ! That goes hand and hand with the senses sight, hearing, touching, smelling, and speaking. If you want to institute punishment for violations, you need to find a solution to make them a better person when they exit.

My solution to tackling solitary confinement is to close them. The Justice Department needs to:

1. Open every file to every inmate in solitary confinement (city and state) especially assault on officer allegations.

2. Ask every inmate in solitary confinement, if received injuries to the body, but threatened or coerced to refuse medical attention.

3. Investigate how many "use of forces" each correction officer involved in these incidents had over a period of 3 years.

4. How many complaints by inmates and their family members, against the Correction Officers involved in these incidents?

5. How many times each Correction Officer appeared in front of the Inspector General and charges were unfounded? Inspector general works hand in hand with the jails.

6. Read every incident report written by Correction and Superior Officers, and look for inconsistencies

7. Investigate the superior officer conducting the hearing and how many inmates they found guilty and the evidence proved they were innocent?

8. Conduct private interviews with every inmate in solitary confinement and each facility, to find out if guards beat them gang style or if they witnessed the gang style beatings on other inmates, and who is the goon squad. Get a bus and take them outside the jails in groups, away from the jails and they will talk.

Last but not least the justice department need to plant investigators posing as inmates in every city and state jail and weed out the corruption overall. These Correction Officers are responsible for the demise of the prison system and with this new breed of inmates. It is not going to end well. The younger generation is not going to stand by and allow correction officers to continuously gang style beat, disrespect them and place them in solitary confinement whereas they are isolated and hungry, no starving, for no reason other than muscle flexing. They are going to fight back and riots will begin to pop up in every jail and prison in New York City and State.

I am fully aware you need a penalized system designed for unruly inmates who have no self-control. You have to distinguish the mentally damaged inmates from the inmates targeted by abuse of power. All others need some sort of boot camp

If inmates are assaulting correction officers, the physical evidence presented to the prosecution should equate an easy conviction. I'm not referring to the Rikers Island Correction Officer who was cut in the face. The prisoners that cut him and his partner who allegedly smuggled in razors should be charged.

The correction department needs to wean out bogus claims by correction officer, who use solitary confinement as a measure to get even with an inmate for being verbally correct or incorrect.

You cannot tell me the proper way to penalize a prisoner is to make them crazier than they were before solitary confinement. The prison system has found a way to justify solitary confinement. To me it is just another Guantanamo Bay, modern day slavery and torture chamber and a reason for racist and prejudice people to slave cage blacks and minorities.

Solitary confinement does not need to be a total isolation of a steel door, a slot and no human contact whatsoever. Close solitary confinement before it is too late. You are creating monsters instead of reforming inmates and unleashing them back into society.

CHAPTER 8

SEX

Rapist, Pimp, Prostitute, Copstitute, Child Molester, Whore, Church Whore, Pedophile, down low brother, Homo, Dyke, Lesbian, Bisexual, Trysexual, Carpet Burner, Skank, Gigolo, Crack whore, Dominatrix, Thot and Dick Sucker. These are just some of the derogatory titles awarded to my colleagues by my colleagues and echoed throughout the prison walls by my co-workers.

We are a quasi-military establishment and should be conducting ourselves in a professional manner. Instead some are gallivanting around wearing their sexuality on their sleeves participating in oral sex, sexual intercourse, orgies, ménage a trios and anal sex, at work, as though we are at the playboy mansion, hotel or an abandon.

In the 80's the sexual appetites of some of my colleagues was blatant and rampant on Rikers Island.

They didn't care where they had sex at in the prisons; basements, slop sinks, officers bathrooms, locker room, stair cases, ranking officers offices and Rikers Island parking lots. Some were so bold they would have sex in the Warden's office, on top of the desk, after the Warden left for the day.

How do I know ? This was the continuous inside chatter among my colleagues . This is the stuff you will never read about or hear about outside the prison walls . Unless you personally know a Correction Officer. Meanwhile, this is what your taxpaying dollars funded.

It was the norm for some female and male officers, to trade sex with ranking officers for non-inmate office positions, easy assignment or transfers off Riker Island to a borough jail or court facility, cars, houses, expensive gifts and money. A female Correction Officer could get very far if her head game was tight.

Inside the prison system, sex is the primary focus for a number of people, from the ranking officers to the prisoners. The prisoners I can understand to a certain degree because they are deprived of access to normal traditional intercourse.

My colleagues on the other hand, have an abundance of access, once they leave the prison walls. They have girlfriends, boyfriends, wives and husbands at home.

There is absolutely no reason to tamper with their colleagues or target every new recruit as a slab of meat or a conquest.

However, sexing a colleagues is one thing, but when you cross the line and have sex with the prisoners. You have crossed over and need to get fitted for the silver bracelets.

I worked in male dominated facilities my entire career it was apparent many male prisoners looked at female correction officers with the same lustful eyes they would look at a female on the street. That is the nature of the beast. That uniform does not stop the Adam and Eve, Yin and Yang philosophy. They are undressing you with their eyes and looking at every nook and cranny of your ass, cookie and tits. It is up to the female in uniform to deter and regulate the male prisoner, by demanding respect and not succumbing to their false sense of flattery and interest. These prisoners don't give a damn about you, same as many male correction officers who have girlfriends and wives at home. They just want the cookie and bragging rights among their male colleagues. They will abandon you for the next new recruit. In both instances, shut it down while you still have an ounce of dignity.

You are about to read some shocking unbelievable tales of the sexual dark forbidden side of care, custody and control. Some of these stories are so dirty and low down they will make you cringe.

This is the section where I deliver some of the disgusting and distasteful sexual behavior allegedly conducted by correction employees. I say allegedly because I definitely was not a spectator at any of these atrocious acts. The language might be a little distasteful. Beware ...

I want you to know exactly what some of these correction officers are engaging in, while they should be doing their jobs. The idle mind is the devil's playground. These Correction Officers below definitely played in the devil's playground.

Most of these cases made headlines in the major newspapers and some of these did not, but it definitely is common knowledge within the correction department. Your taxpaying dollars were paying for some of these Correction Officers to wet their sexual appetites, instead of focusing on their jobs. Once you have sex with an inmate, you lose your dignity and title as a Correction Officer. It is called; sleeping with the enemy.

In the 20 years working with male prisoners, not once did I look at a prisoner and say (like a couple of my female colleagues) "oooh he cute ". To me it is a written and unwritten rule, just like, you do not curse in front of granny. It is an automatic no-no. You do not look at inmates in any way, other than a prisoner trying to escape out of jail. They not your boo or bae.

Well that case has been brought to the attention to every *Correction Officer in the early 80's when a Rikers Island male Correction Officer, engaged in oral sex with a male inmate and the inmate bit his penis off because the officer did not deliver what was promised. The inmate saved the evidence (bit penis) for Department of Investigation Inspector General. I do not know if it was because of the incident, but this officer committed suicide years later.

*Another incident allegedly occurred in a court facility. A senior male Correction Officer, opened the cell to a segregated homosexual inmate, put a condom on and forced anal sex upon the inmate. He ejaculated took the condom off and threw it. The inmate saved the evidence for Department of Investigation Inspector General. I do not know what happened to the correction officer. I hear he retired shortly thereafter

*The female officer who leased or utilized her home in Queens New York, every year, two weeks before Christmas to a bunch of Correction Warden, Deputy Wardens, Captains to have a big ass orgy sex party filled with alcohol, weed, cocaine and live sex shows. She charged admission. The problem here is illegal drug use among primarily ranking officers.

*According to the New York Post, Correction Officer Andrea Buchanan, 30, was arrested on September 20, 2011 and charged with sexual misconduct, forcible touching and official misconduct. She was caught having sex with an inmate prisoner at the Eric M. Taylor Center

* According to the New York Daily News, Correction Officer Clara Espada, 41, pleaded guilty on March 8, 2012 to third degree bribe receiving, a felony, and misdemeanor forcible touching. She was prosecuted for having sex with a male prisoner three times and smuggling drugs, cigarettes and alcohol into the George Motchan Detention Center at Rikers. As part of a plea agreement, Espada is expected to receive a six-month sentence plus probation.

*"According to the New York Daily News and New York Correction Officer Marlie Meme 37 who worked at f Anna M Kross Center (C-95) on Rikers Island, filed a lawsuit against the city and Captain John Rudolph.. Instead of supervising her he was trying to get into her panties. His pickup lines included. "When you gonna give me some? What breast-size you have? You have small tits or big ones. She said the moment she started working at this Rikers island jail Captain John Rudolph became a sexual predator. The last straw was when he grabbed, groped her breast, humiliated her by ripping her shirt buttons, and pulled her on top of him, right in the front of another officer, in full view of the inmates. Once she made a complaint, she stated the officers retaliated. I find that hard to believe, not my colleagues, they stick together. Just bullshitting, of course they retaliated. That is how it was and probably

still is. I heard through the grapevine she won her case and he had to pay her and she quit. I think he retired. That is a criminal act. That falls into the sexual section of the law. If a civilian does this, they are charged as a sex offender. Why wasn't he arrested?

* According to the New York Post, Correction Officer Yolanda Dickinson, who worked at Rikers from 1997 to 2004, proudly penned a book about her fair share of dalliances with inmates. She admitted she met a Rikers inmate on her watch, a gang member from her neighborhood who had admitted to killing a rapist; also, the father of her 17-year-old son served 10 years in federal prison on drug charges. She was fired for "undue familiarity" in 2004, after an inmate called her from Rikers.

*According to the New York Daily News, Correction Officer Doreen Baker, 39, may be fired for carrying on an "improper relationship" with a 39-year-old inmate identified only as "Hunter," when she supervised his work detail. Investigators say Hunter called Baker more than 170 times while in jail, and then moved in with her after his release in March 2008.

* According to the New York Post, In 2008 Correction Officer Kadessha Mulgrav was under investigation for a secret midnight stroll to the Rikers Island inmate shower room to have sex with inmate Lee Woods who is an accused cop killer and he was caught with handcuff key. She is beyond disgusting.

* In an alleged July 2008 rape case reported by The Village Voice on August 5, 2008, the alleged victim claimed, "that someone entered her cell in the 1,000-bed Rose M. Singer Center while she was asleep, sometime before 6 a.m. on July 3. She says the intruder (or intruders) bound and gagged her with bed sheets and then used a dildo-like object to sexually assault her. Other inmates may have acted as lookouts during the alleged assault. The female inmate, who was being held on grand-larceny charges for the past three months, was discovered at about 6 a.m. by an Officer and a Captain who were touring the building. The Officer saw her lying on her back on the floor of her cell, blindfolded with bed sheets wrapped around her neck, mouth, and legs. The incident was reported to central command at 7:30 a.m., and the female inmate was transported to the Elmhurst Hospital Center. The major question

was, how this alleged sexual assault happened and the inmate did not share her cell with anyone. Officials won't talk about the investigation, and there's no word on whether any arrests have been made."

* Allegedly a male correction officer who worked in OBCC the solitary confinement, disciplinary jail on Rikers Island would instead of just serving breakfast through the slot on the inmates door. The inmates would put their penises on the food slot so the correction officer could suck their penises along with serving them breakfast, of course for favors in return. The person that told me the story was a witness to this correction officer's sexual activities. He said he did not realize what was going on until he zoomed in. He said, "What is this dick for breakfast? " This correction officer is disgusting

* In the 80's the midnight tour was the party tour. Countless correction officers came to work on the midnight tour, to get high, fuck and sleep in that nasty dirty building. It was a regular occurrence when

I am at a loss for words. Even now, I am trying to comprehend the deviant behavior and mindset of these correction officers. Yes, care, custody and control are the blueprint. However, the caring aspects are criminal. This has nothing to do with supervision. This risky behavior and crossing boundaries is deep rooted. They need a nice comfortable cell and isolation so they can sort things out. I think Correction Officers should focus more on their jobs, than their sexual appetite. Its understandable relationships are formed at any workplace because it is like your second home. It is great if you have a healthy sexual appetite. However, when a Correction Officer crosses the line and has sex at work with an employee or the inmates, there is something morally and legally wrong.

CHAPTER 9

DRUGS

Correction Officers back in the 80's loved to self medicate; with crack-cocaine, cocaine, heroin, weed, blunts, and alcohol. They were very vocal about their love for that nose candy and weed. In 1983 when I joined the department, there was no random drug testing. The only way you could get drug tested is if a ranking officer had it out for you, or someone called inspector general to report you were getting high off drugs.

Oh, it was not just the Correction Officers getting high. The ranking officers were, too. I am talking Captains, Assistant Deputy Wardens and the Wardens; there was no random testing for ranking officers back then either.

During my tenure, I never saw anyone actually getting high, with the exception of the correction and ranking officers lighting up weed, after exiting the Rikers Island Bridge. You knew they were smoking weed; because the hand placement and smell was dead giveaways. If you lowered your window, you could get a whiff of the weed.

I have seen the effects of drugs on many of my colleagues, primarily my sister. Her introduction to crack cocaine was delivered by a soulless colleague in blue. Drugs, drugs and more drugs in the NYC & NYS prison system.

Drugs is big business and rampant; within the prison system. Inmates and officers alike are looking to capitalize off it. It is my belief that drugs is the root of many problems inside and outside the prison system. Many crimes revolve around drugs, from using it, selling it, possessing it, assaulting for it, or killing for it. There are so many people in jail today because of the drug factor.

It is unfortunate when you have Correction Officers who are using, smuggling and selling drugs to inmates within the city and state prisons. The sad part is they are so quick to call an inmate a scum bag and talk down to them. However, they are just as criminal.

To add insult to injury; these Correction Officers do not have a problem encouraging and selling crack cocaine to their colleagues. They will get their own co-workers hooked on drugs so they can collect money from them every time they are paid. Look into the Rikers Island parking lot. How many expensive cars do you see? If these officers are not doing a lot of overtime, working a side job or came into an inheritance, how can they afford these cars.

After they began drug testing correction officers, it is my opinion that 50% of Correction and ranking officers became alcoholics. They will not admit it and yes, it is legal. Nevertheless, when you are working under the influence, your judgment is off. There were many violent drunks in the correction department and these are your potential inmate and colleague physical and sexual abusers. Some of these officers come to work drunk and angry ready to beat somebody down. Alternatively, they want a drink and are agitated because their alcoholic asses have to wait until their shift ends, before they can blow their livers out.

The bar scene is the first thing that the new recruits are introduced to. The goal after every tour, especially the 4x12 tour it to hit the bar scene and drive home drunk. What that rookie needs to be careful is they are on their way to becoming alcoholics. They will soon find themselves saying, "I need a drink" and I need a drink will be their medicine to function.

Now, that the media is finally reporting the rampant circulation of drugs and corruption throughout the prison system. We now know; the Correction Officers were and are bringing it in, or allowing clearance for it to enter the facilities. They wrote glorifying books about it.

I am reading these newspapers and the Commissioners, Mayors and Governors are or many placing sole blame on the inmate visitors, and are now trying to penalize the visitors by limiting inmate contact with their family members and eventually end visits for prisoners totally; via video conference. The administration has no idea what they are doing by implementing a policy as such. The inmates will become extremely agitated and hostile and eventually a bloodbath will ensue. That will create an escalated hostile environment, for Correction Officers that are not part of the drug smuggling and corruption.

It is obvious these admin folk have never worked in the prison system. When you can sit in the belly of the beast with these inmates, like the honest professional correction officers do. Only then will you have a better understanding of how you should proceed.

Okay so, what do you do to the correction officers who are primarily responsible for drugs entering the facilities? Do you take away their badges? On the other hand, do you continue to turn a blind eye that the culprit really is, one of your own? There is no way an inmate can get pounds of weed, large quantities of cocaine, and alcohol in the jail without the assistance of a correction officer, and a superior officers covering for them. Every time something goes wrong, stop blaming just the slaves, excuse me I mean prisoners. It is the New York City Department of Corrections fault these drugs are getting in the prisons and it is time to do the job you were hired to do.

The finale of it all is, when you have a bunch of people who are supposed to be police-ing the jails mimicking the corner drug dealer is. You are fighting a losing battle. Imitation is the highest form of flattery to a prisoner. The prisoners have no respect for any type of authority you inflict, and you cannot lead by example. When prisoners learn you were arrested in a crack house in your pajamas, you cannot lead by example, and your colleagues cannot trust you.

When ex-convicts ride the Rikers Island 101 bus, to meet you in the Rikers

Island officer's parking lot, to drop off drugs to you, in uniform, before you enter the building. You cannot lead by example. You are consciously walking onto Rikers Island with every intention of distributing drugs to prisoners and possibly your colleagues, placing everyone's life in danger. Prisoners getting high in a confined environment can trigger a negative effect.

Correction Officers dealing drugs for what? Extra money? We are paid a lot of money to just baby-sit. ? In addition, there is plenty of overtime, why not work extra hours. That is a character issue.

Gary Heyward a former correction officer sold drugs because. Why? He was an addict. I do not remember hearing about any addictions. An addiction would explain a senseless act like bringing drugs into jail facility, to place your colleagues' lives in a danger. Nevertheless, I do recall reading about child support, and no stability financially. Really? There were and are plenty of men paying child support or supporting their children. They work extra shifts and side jobs. It was rough but they managed.

Do not get me wrong, I am all for redemption. However, then I read an article in the daily news about former jailed guard Gary Heyward who smuggled drugs, alcohol and cigarettes. The tip of the iceberg was a prisoners grandmother sucked his penis, in his van, because she came up short on her $500 red velvet cake and liquor bottle; to get to her grandson, in jail for his birthday. I was sickened. As a Correction Officer and formerly in the military, he was wrong on so many levels. It is a disgraceful character and moral issue all the way to the soul. It comes from a place of darkness. I expect that from a common criminal because many of them move without a soul.

There are also many Correction Officers past and probably present, who work in the court facilities, which can go out of the buildings for lunch. Instead of going to pick up a meal, they go to bars to drink and sniff, their lunch away. We call it liquid lunches. They have to be alcoholics and drug addicts if they cannot wait until their shift ends. These are your DUI- DWI stars. They most likely wear their uniform home so if they are stopped. The cops let them go as a courtesy. I worked with many correction officers reeking of new alcohol. They claim, they random drug test, but from what I learned in the past is, the city cannot afford to random drug test because it is too costly.

They need to random drug test and use breathalyzers frequently to wean out the bad seeds. These Correction and ranking officers are problematic to the well being of the department. I guaranteed you a large percentage of these characters are behind the demise of the correction department and today its worst. Get rid of them. They are killing reform.

Below are a couple of incidents I heard during my tenure. I am quite sure there are many more but they were covered up.

* As a rookie in 1983 , while working on Rikers Island in The Eric M Taylor Center formerly known as New York City Correction Institution for Men (C-76), 1983-1984 a Hispanic Correction Officer was allegedly arrested at roll call for having 4 kilo's of cocaine taped to his body under his uniform shirt. I worked with this officer on the midnight tour several times. He was a nice guy but made me extremely nervous. He had no problem sleeping in a comatose state, with his mouth wide open, while supposedly watching the inmates; in the dorm area he worked. After his arrest, I understood why he was so comfortable. He was a drug-pushing dealer in blue.

*Subsequently in the 80's a popular Warden, was driving a vehicle pulled over and allegedly the police found a couple of kilos of cocaine. The authorities swept it under the rug.

 *The Assistant Deputy Warden who would have weekend cocaine parties at his home. Special invited guest Captains Deputy Wardens and Wardens.

*The Correction Officer hanging out, in a crack house in smoking crack, not a care in the world. Long and behold the crack house is raided and they were arrested. How they was able to maneuver out of it is a mystery, but they remained on the job and retired with full pension.

*The Correction Officers who drove to work and parked in the officer's parking lot. They were greeted by the local drug dealer. Probably an inmate they babysat on Rikers Island. The drug buy took place right in the Rikers Island parking lot. The officer got drugs in exchange for money. The drug dealer would wait for the Rikers Island City bus (101) and either gets off at the foot of the bridge to an awaiting vehicle. Or transfer to public transportation.

*The Correction Officers who drove to Rikers Island in uniform, with drugs in their cars, so if the police stop them, they will not search the car.

The list goes on and on.

CHAPTER 10

NEW YORK'S BOLDEST THUGS

When I was a rookie working on Rikers Island, I saw some of the most horrific unwarranted beatings by my male colleagues. I saw most of my white male colleagues quick to beat up a black inmate and my black male colleagues quick to join in to fit in. What a bunch of losers. Some of these prisoners did absolutely nothing wrong, or something so minute. Meanwhile they were brutally beaten gang style.

"This country was built on gangs. I think this country is still run on gangs. Republicans, Democrats, the police department, the FBI, the CIA...those are gangs, the correctional officers. I had a correctional officer tell me "we the biggest gang in New York State". This was a quote I found online by rapper Tupac Shakar. This is what he was told by a state correction officer.

Its amazing prison guards have a problem with the blood and crypts, but the only difference between a prison guard and gang member is guards hide behind their badges to assault and murder inmates. They are protected by their superior officers, who in turn commit federal crimes, by falsifying legal documents, to cover up excessive force, and cover their ranking position at the same time.

We witnessed it right with the arrest of Ex-Police Chief James Burke of Suffolk County.

He was accused and convicted of beating heroin addict Christopher Loeb, who broke in his car stealing a duffel bag stuffed with cigars, pornographic DVD's and sex toys from Mr. Burke's police car.. Burke admitted to torturing handcuff prisoner after prisoner called him a pervert.. According to the NY Times; Burke "went out of control screaming and cursing at Loeb and assaulting him until a detective finally said, "Boss, that's enough, that's enough" Burke pressured the detectives who witnessed the assault to conceal it. The feds eventually stepped in and prison will be his home.

The bottom line is no matter how you dress it up and change the name, the beat up squad that they have in every jail is the definition of a gang. These brutal Guantanamo Bay like Correction Officers are a bunch of hooligan criminals. They have them in the city and state correction department.

A Correction Officer's shield and identification card does not give them the license to beat an inmate to a pulp because he did not look forward, made eye contact with an officer, or checked an officer when they called them nigger or spic.

If you are arrested and sent to Rikers Island, if you are not personally beaten by the correction officers, you will definitely witness correction officers conducting gang style beatings on another prisoner. If you are lucky, you might even catch a correction officer beating a colleague.

Without a doubt many male officers in New York City & State Correction Officers have a severe problem controlling their egos and hands.

There is a serious slave mentality in the world whereas people's first reaction to rectifying a situation is physical violence. The art of beating a person, who they believed misbehaved, is common. This type of response has been passed down, from correction officers generation to generation until it has become the norm. Not just on the job but in their personal lives too. You often hear people, not just in the black communities' say, "Yeah when I was younger, my parents used to whip my ass if I got out of line". As an adult, some of us used that same concept when it came to our children. If they act up, we will beat their asses and keep them in line. It's learned mimicked behavior from our upbringing. .

On the other hand, the art of visual threatening and intimidation was a factor "You know when your mother just gave you that look, like you better not act up or your ass is grass. Well the same thing happens with male Correction Officers. The only difference is these prisoners are not your children. They are grown ups. How humiliating it must be, to fear a correction officer and you are doing nothing wrong.

There are many loose violent cannons in the correction department, who come to work angry, looking to flex their muscles, and start shit. They feel they need to illustrate who is superior with that bullying I will kick your ass attitude, looking for a victim. I mean really. Who fights past adolescent years?

While some of my male colleagues were trying to impress female correction officers; what they failed to realize is, many of the female officers had a running joke. The male colleagues and superior officer, who come to work on that rah rah shit, bossing people around; were wimps at home because their wives were running the show, or they had little penises and or the napoleon syndrome. Where they thought they were impressing the female officers, we would chuckle and look at them with disgust.

Some of these female officers and female superior officers, are just as bad and stupid at the same time. Especially when going up against a male prisoner. They come to work with an attitude. They may have their menstrual , hangover or significant other issues.

A prisoner asks them for a phone call, toilet paper or something they are entitled to, and their response is either "Don't ask me for shit", or "Get the fuck out my face", while they sit at their desk stuffing their faces or taking a nap. If the prisoners addresses the disrespect, they may in return get the other prisoners, who get special privileges by them, to beat that prisoner up. My thing is what the hell you come to work for, that's part of your job. They wonder why somewhere down the line, they are knocked the hell out by a prisoner.

Male Correction Officers definitely like to bully, beat and intimidate female Correction Officers. I know that because I was a victim of physical abuse by Correction Officer James Carter in 1984, and have the document to prove it. I do not know what was in his head but it is my opinion he wanted sex from me and was angry because I never paid him any attention. He probably wanted to be the one to tell his boys he hit it first. You know like a conqueror.

Did he actually think sniffing my seat on the Rikers Island bus was going to do the trick? When I saw that I knew he was a pathetic disgusting pervert. Who sniffs a seat on a public bus.

He was a well-liked senior officer and instead of taking me under his wing and protecting me. He became abusive and attacked me at work because I asked him a simple question. "Are you relieving me for meal?" Let the inmates relieve you was not the proper response. Yes, my response was childish. However, it did not constitute fracturing my finger and bruising my chin. Nor did it constitute the administration covering it up. What a loser and coward. Grown ass men should know better.

Let me give you an example of the demeanor of some of these loose cannon correction officers. This has nothing to do with care, custody and control.

Example; if an inmate says "Good morning officer" they will respond with "What the fuck you say asshole" if the inmate responds with" Damn officer, all I did was say good morning, you don't have to disrespect me,. I'm a grown ass man." That is an automatic beat down.

The correction officer's reason will probably be, he does not want inmates to say shit to him, period, point blank. The correction officer who started it will probably tell the captain this guy is an asshole. The inmate will be all bloodied and bruised. They will write an infraction and injury report. The inmate will probably never make it to the clinic because they will have him sign a medical refusal, to cover their tracks. On the other hand, they will skip the infraction and tell him when he gets to the clinic, he better say he fell in the shower, or they will be back to whip his ass. This is uncalled for and all of that could have been avoided.

All correction officers receive the same type of training, including use of force training. Nowhere in the use of force playbook does it state to use force if an inmate curses you out. You are supposed to use your pen, not your fist, feet, gas or batons. If an inmate strikes you that is a different story, but there still is a limit.

All of the city and state correctional facilities have institutional goon squads. If they have a problem with an inmate, or simply do not like them, or just looking to get their jollies off , like they are in public school, the goon squad will pay them an unforgettable visit, and they will become a casualty.

During 1983-1984, I personally witnessed some of the most horrific beatings any human being should have to endure, while working at the Eric M Taylor Center formerly known as the C-76 New York City Correctional Institution for Men. I can still visualize and replay some of those beatings placed upon inmates and what surprises me is the inmates did not die. I do not know the condition they are in today, but mental illness or paralysis, sticks in the forefront of my mind. When you are constantly beat on your head, your brain has to suffer damage.

I would watch the beatings and the cover-up machine instituted immediately. A pen and piece of paper goes a long way. The sad part is many of the superior officers assist in these cover-ups to avoid demotion and lawsuits.

The one beating in particular; has stuck in my head and still haunts me to this day. It was the vicious beating I saw inflicted upon this inmate they called "Dead Eye". The name speaks for itself; one of his eyes was dead. He was an adolescent inmate. He was loud and to me harmless. He probably was a pain in the ass to some Correction Officers. I do not fully know his history but I do know that in my care and custody, listened to me, and followed my rules.

On this particular morning, I was already working the midnight to morning shift. I was assigned; by myself to escort approximately 100 inmates to breakfast; to the institutional mess hall that was in another part of the building. It was approximately 5am.

In formation, we were walking down the corridor. I was watching and counting my prisoners. As we got a few steps from the big mess hall, a Correction Officer pulled my adolescent inmate called "Dead Eye" off the line. A bunch of correction officers commenced to beating his ass. I was stunned and horrified. They pulled out these long black flashlights, and were hitting him on top of his head. I saw blood gushing out the top of his head. A gang of correction officers joined in, just for the hell of it, kicking and punching this inmate; as he lay on the floor motionless. He never fought back.

I did not understand why they were beating him and it scared the hell out of me. Instinctively I knew to keep quiet. As a Correction Officer, if you speak out against this type of behavior, retaliation is in order. You might be set-up or possibly fired. That is why a correction officer does not speak out against this type of gang style beatings. I later learned this Correction Officer that instituted these type of gang style beatings, had a lot of clout, all the way to the Mayor's office. This officer furthered his career and I honestly believe I would not be receiving my pension had I filed any complaints against them.

That day changed my approach to dealing with prisoners. I would always warn them the possible repercussions of acting out. I warned them some officers were just looking for a reason to fuck them up so listen and keep quiet, that they have no wins. At the end of the day, I always kept in mind every prisoner is someone's child, and I was not going to be part of no cover-ups. Nor was I going to lie under oath. I needed my job. Look at the correction Officers now who partook in gang style beating cover-up. Some are fired or in jail or both.

The beatings were rampant in the jail I worked in on Rikers Island. The beatings were not as bad once I left Rikers Island and worked in the borough houses and court divisions.

I do not think these type of correction officers need anger management. They need to be fired and jailed. Assault is a felonious crime. If a person beats someone in the street, they are arrested, and charged with a crime. These correction officers need to be, held accountable for their actions. At the end of the day, it is costing the taxpayers a lot of money. These prisoners are suing them left and right now. Who do you think is footing the bill ? We all are. Yes, the taxpaying public; its coming out of your check every time you get paid. These are some expensive ass whipping. If you do not care about prisoners on Rikers Island, you should at least care about paying for a gang style beating by correction officers you were not, at least privy to see.

They are putting a lot of focus on New York City Police Officers. What about the assaults on Rikers Island? More importantly what about the assaults and unreported murders in the New York State Jails? I have heard many stories about abuse in New York State prisons

I said it once and I will say it again. There are innocent till proven guilty people in Rikers Island; only accused of a crime, not yet convicted.. They are entitled to have their day in court in front of a judge and jury.

A Correction Officer's first course of action should not be deadly physical force. You have never heard of a Correction Officer dying in the line of duty like police officers. Pay close attention because its about to happen. It is my opinion this new breed of prisoners entering the system are not going to sit back and be disrespected by a blue shirt, especially for no reason. They will start applying that same deadly physical force upon Correction Officers. It is already starting to happen. Correction Officers must remember , they are only part of a gang inside. Once they leave work, they are not part of a gang. These blood and crypts are gang affiliates and family inside and out of prison. They do a lot of recruiting on Rikers Island and the New York State prisons. They are not as stupid as you think they are. Many survived the streets. If you read, further on the site below. A blog gang banger has already penned a Rikers officer hit list.

According to Correctionone.com

Inmate assaults on uniformed staff resulting in serious injuries have nearly doubled, from 25 to 46, over the first nine months of this fiscal year compared with the same period last year, sources told the Daily News. That includes inmate Daquan Monroe, 18, who repeatedly punched a correction officer in the face at the jail's Robert N. Davoren Center last Oct. 13, video footage recently obtained by The News shows.

"It's happening more frequently, and something has to be done to stop it," said Norman Seabrook, president of the Correction Officers

Benevolent Association. "If something isn't done, someone will pay the ultimate price."

Below are some of the headlines the jail guard thugs at work.

Rikers Guards Who Hogtied, Beat Mentally Ill Man May Actually Be Fired

Rikers Island inmate says guard ordered prisoners to attacked him with boiling water & oil

James Parker, 40, said he suffered third-degree burns on his face and upper body from the May 30 attack that a jail guard allegedly ordered. He filed papers asking a judge for permission to file a civil claim against the city.

*The FBI has quietly arrested a city correction officer in what sources said is the start of criminal charges against jail guards suspected of assaulting inmates in a special Rikers Island jail. The sources said federal and Bronx prosecutors have targeted as many as 36 correction officers, including 15 captains and an assistant deputy warden, who worked in the Central Punitive Segregation Unit, a maximum security jail for the city's most violent inmates. City attorneys have also notified 43 officers, including six captains and several wardens, that they will not represent them in court. Criminal indictments, which the sources said could come within weeks, would rock the city Department of Correction. "This is monumental," said Pete Meringolo, head of the Correction Captains Association. "I've been here 24 years and never seen anything like it.

Correction Officer Roger Johnson (No relation to the DA) was the first arrested. He was picked up by federal authorities on Jan. 11 and charged with civil rights violations for the alleged December 1992 beating of an inmate in the segregation unit, known to inmates as the Bing. The officer pleaded not guilty and was released on bond. He faces a court appearance this week. Johnson, the Bronx DA, declined to discuss the charges. The complaint described a system of threats and beatings by guards, often for minor infractions or perceived insults that began the moment an inmate entered the unit. According to the lawsuit, inmates were often stripped, beaten and threatened with additional violence unless they reported their injuries as accidents. Prisoners suffered injuries that included broken jaws and perforated eardrums to permanent disabilities, the complaint charged. Meringolo said his union argued from "day one" that the segregation unit was a bad idea because it isolated the worst prisoners in one location

There has to be many cases in New York City and State correction, whereas inmates that died either at the hands or due to the negligence of Correction Officers and it was covered up. If your family member was murdered in jail, seriously hurt by correction officers, there is a chance you may never find out. On the other hand, by the time you find out, an autopsy cannot be performed, so you have to believe what they tell you the reason is for their death. I would say that would happen more so in New York State Correctional facilities. They have a great cover-up system when they injure you or a family member.

Its common practice that city and state guards will jump you, beat you badly, make you refuse medical treatment, and so the injuries are not documented, and falsify documents and write you assaulted them. They will send you to solitary confinement and you will not be allowed a phone call. They will monitor your outgoing mail, so if you try to tell a family member, that mail will never reach them.

I know first hand because I witnessed these acts on Rikers Island and I have a nephew currently incarcerated in a New York State facility. I saw first hand how they utilized the correction officer cover-up playbook.

It is my opinion it may already be too late, especially if the correction officers continue use deadly physical as an alternative to utilizing their professional communication skills. These inmates are growing tired and numb to the beatings. The only way to stop an inmate if he snaps is to kill them before they kill you. Terrible lack of logic, and terrible results.

CHAPTER 11

COBA NORMAN SEABROOK

COBA stands for the Correction Officers Benevolent Association; Norman Seabrook is the President of the union. He is supposed to be there to protect the correction officers and allegedly gets paid an extra $300,000 a years to do so. However, that was not always the case with my union.

Norman Seabrook is the face of the correction officers and his conduct reflects our image. If he is perceived as a, thief and disrespectful thug, that is not a good presentation.

He represents approximately 11,000 Correction Officers. Norman helped my generation get the 20 years pension back, amongst other things. However, Correction Officers need to keep in mind; Norman knows he is not going to be in that president slot forever. He is still a correction officer, so everything he does with the contract negotiation benefits him to a certain degree. He will sacrifice and throw newly hired Correction Officers under the bus, during contract negotiations, as long as it doesn't affect him.

I know we need unions and its better to have someone represent you but I do not trust my union at all. If you have a problem with another correction officer they will not help you; if you are not part of their clique. If you are a female is being sexually harassed by a male ranking officer, who is politically connected, they will not help you. The politics of it all will not allow you to get the proper help from your union representative in your facility. They either are scared, told to leave it alone or do not care and will leave a correction officer high and dry to fend for themselves.

I have an unfavorable opinion of many of the union representatives, I observed during the course of my career. Some were ringleaders for gang-style inmate beatings, gossipers, cliquish and definitely not a good representative.

I received no assistance whatsoever from my union representatives when I was assaulted at work by a male Correction Officer. In fact; looking back on that incident in 1984, my union representative never reached out to me to see if I was ok.

Nevertheless, in early 2000, I filed an EEOC case against my superior officer in Brooklyn Court Facility for denying me a position I was entitled to. I filed it alone and won before I retired. It never crossed my mind to contact him for help. At that point I was fed up with my union and correction department overall.

I met Norman a couple of times, just briefly. Seem like a cool person. It was early in his career so I guess he was genuine. As the years have gone by, he always struck as the type of guy who wanted to be a celebrity rock star, I mean really famous, I don't blame him, the limelight and the podium can be rather addicting. He has gained enormous power throughout the years and it obvious by some of his actions; it has gone to his head.

Some men are ego driven and sometimes they forget their sweet beginnings, when they were still wet behind the ears, and eager to make a difference. I think that has happened with Norman.

My only problem with Norman is when I retired in 2005, on half pay, I was supposed to receive a variable supplement every year to supplement my income. Instead I didn't receive my money until 10 years later. Meanwhile, Norman makes 300,000 a year plus his Correction Officer salary. What happened to our money we were promised upon retirement Norman?

Throughout the years, I have been hearing all sorts of negative things about Norman Seabrook. His reputation went from bad to worse during the years. People refer to him as the powerful thug, who is politically savvy and intimidating.

It's sad when you have Commissioner Martin Horn who served the department from 2003-2009, state" his wardens believe Norman was more important to their career that he was". That speaks volumes.

I am fully aware that when you are in the position of power, people will make up all sorts of things. However, from what I am reading on social media, and media overall, is that Norman has turned into a bombastic paranoid, vindictive bully.

There was an article in the NY Times stating, "Mr. Seabrook is a volatile personality. He has dined with mayors and shouted in their faces.

One minute he can be heard exclaiming, "God is good," the next unleashing a stream of vulgarities. He once arrived at the home of a senior city official, during contract negotiations, with a pistol strapped to his hip. That's gangster.

The Times spoke with about a dozen current and former senior city officials, both inside and outside the department, who have dealt with him regularly over the years and were privately critical of him but almost no one would be quoted discussing Mr. Seabrook, citing concerns that he could sabotage their careers.

Some also expressed fears about their safety while visiting Rikers, worrying that a correction officer might look the other way if an inmate suddenly got violent.

According to the article, one of his main targets was Investigator Florence Finkle, a female investigator who came to the New York City Department of Corrections in 2010, to clean up this mess and by 2012 she was ousted and replaced by Norman Seabrook's childhood friend Michael Blake.

Ms. Finkle spent roughly two decades investigating misconduct by the police, including serving as executive director of the Civilian Complaint Review Board, which provides oversight for the Police Department. This woman has a no nonsense approach to getting rid of waste in law enforcement. That is exactly what New York City Department of Correction needs.

Nevertheless, Norman Seabrook did everything in his power to get rid of investigator Florence Finkle even though the correction department desperately needed her. He transferred her top people, called for her resignation, denounced her on your weekly radio show and eventually got his wish when she was forced out.

If this article is in fact true, that's hood, even for you Norman, and if it is factual, your actions reflect that of an abusive womanizing bully. That abusive behavior is indicative of what many women in the correction department face on a daily basis by their male colleagues.

If we do not dance to their music, and go along with their program, they try everything in their power to get rid of us, or make our lives a living hell.

I for one definitely suffered at the hands of my male colleagues for not going along with his little program.

Norman baby, you know, just as I knew, what the hell has been going on, on Rikers Island and throughout the correction department. The only difference between back then and now; the media is reporting it.

You joined the force two years after me, and it is our generation, and our culture, that set the blue print for the demise of the correction department. You know it has gotten worse and you saw the violence first hand and may, or may not have participated in it.

It is my opinion that Norman Seabrook has been and is part of the problem, and does not want to fix it. When Norman Seabrook covers up for correction officers that will, beat an inmate, fracturing his nose and eye sockets, and his defense is, they defended themselves and did everything that they were supposed to do. You know that is a crock of shit.

You know first hand some of these Correction Officers are loose cannon and will damn near kill these inmates.

If an unfortunate circumstance happened to your child and they were incarcerated and beat to a pulp, by correction officers, would that type of excessive force would be condoned?

Would you want a person like Investigator Florence Finkle to do her job and get down to the root of the problem and find prosecute these correction officers? This type of excessive force has been going on since the beginning of time and it needs to stop.

Remember this Mr. Seabrook; all good things come to an end. What goes up must come down and judging on the history of COBA, I can almost guarantee a front-page scandal of you Norman Seabrook. It will be your own people to bring you down and sell you down the river. That crab in the basket syndrome still exists and I know you stepped on many toes. These white and black folks do not like you. For your sake, I hope you are squeaky clean, but who is, with that much power. It is time to retire and enjoy the rest of your life before you wind up behind bars as a fluke.

CHAPTER 12

NYS GREENHAVEN CORRECTIONAL FACILITY

This chapter is near and dear to my heart. I decided to include this chapter after the Correction Officers at New York State Greenhaven Correctional Facility decided to gang style/attempt murder on my nephew Delamar Brown .

You are about to read a series of letters I wrote when this incident occurred last year. My cries for help primarily went on deaf ears. What a horrible world we live in. Norman Siegel said it best "PEOPLE DON'T CARE". Instead of Acting Commissioner Anthony Annucci and Governor Cuomo looking into the matter, they swept under the rug. When I called State Inspector General to inform them they used excessive force on my nephew for no reason. He told me to hold on and came back to the phone and said. "Oh he assaulted an officer". After months of writing letters and weekly visits. I had to finally got an FBI Agent on the phone to get some action. He sent the Inspector General and dude interviewed my nephew . The inspector general told him he was not going to win his hearing, nobody does. With all of the evidence of misconduct and correction officers testimony in my favor, equipped with no injuries to any correction officer. That was his response. I told him straight out I do not trust him because I see how city Inspector General gets down. He tried to act as if he was really going to investigate. He was just as full of shit as everyone else. My nephew is not the only one they are torturing at Greenhaven Correctional facility. Guantanamo Bay is in full effect and their goon squad is a bunch of racist White and Hispanic Correction Officers acting like its hunting season when they come to work / I want answers why my nephew has sat in solitary confinement for a year for assault on officer and that is a blatant lie and the Correction Officers were allowed to get away with it.

These letters were written in haste. These are however official documents. Disregard typos and misspelled words, and recognize fear, anger and disgust.

December 6, 2014

Subject: Green Haven Correction Officers Attempt Murder on Delamar Brown

Dear Attorney General Eric Holder,

UPDATE: December 6, 2014 This is an update to the document I faxed yesterday. I spoke to State Inspector General James Cross prior to forwarding this document to him. As I stated I do not know who is in bed with these superior officers at Green Haven and yesterday confirmed it. I was informing him about misconduct and he was adamant about my nephew assaulting the officers. However, the reality is they attempted murder on his life. He basically had his mind made up. He needs to be investigated as well. When inspector general is corrupt there is nothing anyone can do. I now know for a fact the beatings in Green Haven are common. Its time for someone to investigate this jail and if something else happens to my nephew, and nothing has been done to rectify the situation at this jail. I will hold everyone accountable. I also learned the reason for the set-up and beating is probably because Captain Cary and his colleagues are upset I am publishing a book about the corruption I saw in the NYC Correction Dept. They have still not released his property to him, he needs his personal items and law work, and they probably damaged it. Someone needs to interview every single inmate. I also learned there was a superior officer present when they were beating him to a pulp and he did say he wants no part of it, they were not following procedures, and for the officers to clean this up. I am getting calls everyday from prisoner's family members about this incident. Someone needs to keep an eye on the cameras in his cell area to also see if they drugged his food, so they can get his DNA on the officer's finger to solidify their actions. My nephew did not assault those officers. He is not a mentally disturbed person. Only a mentally disturbed person would fight a gang of officers with sticks. He also was forced to submit to an AIDS test so they could cover their actions. Why would he refuse medical treatment but submit to an AIDS Test. That doesn't add up. They attempted murder and violated his rights by forcing him. I want these bogus jail charges dropped and these officers brought up on attempted murder charges. If an inmate attempts murder on an officer they will be brought up on charges. They also need to be brought up on departmental charges for falsifying documents. All the officers on duty that day need to be questioned by the Justice Department and if they lie. They need to be fired. If my nephew is not vindicated, I am prepared to go to every news station and take every legal measure until Green Haven is held accountable for brutally beating inmate unjustly.

December 5, 2014

Dear Attorney General Eric Holder,

My name is Robin Kay Miller. I am a retired New York City Correction Officer. Yesterday I visited my nephew Delamar Brown 06B2999 at Green Haven Correctional Facility. Right now I am submitting this document and I do not have time for typos, proofreading, and spell check or to correctly spell these State Correction Officer names correctly. I pray to God my nephew Delamar Brown is not dead already or in a coma. The Correction Officers, Captain and Sergeant has attempted murder on my nephew's life on Saturday November 29, 2014. All of them should be charged with attempted murder. There is no way I will be able to contact him because he has been placed in the Solitary Confinement and makes no phone calls and gets one visit a week. They will not give him his property or his law work. They are tampering with his food or not feeding him. He is horribly skinny and withdrawn. He could barely walk; he is limping from the bruises on his thigh and leg. His neck is swollen and shoulder is hurting and to cover their tracks. They made him basically sign a medical refusal, to disable him from getting medical attention. He needs medical attention ASAP. He needs to be removed from that facility immediately or he might wind up dead by means of State Correction Officers and State Correction Sergeants and State Correction Captain Cary.

I am afraid because his life is in jeopardy by the people who are supposed to protect him.

Correction Officers Cefaloni, Sergeants Merigold, Ragloon or Mulligani and CAPTAIN DANIEL CARY MEAN BUSINESS. They have not only violated their rules and regulations. They have violated the human rights of my nephew Delamar Brown. I do not want another Eric Garner situation. He is being penalized for something he did not do and when he requested to bring in witnesses to the keep lock hearing he was cursed out by Lieutenant Murphy, beat up tortured by Correction Cefaloni and his goon squad and placed in solitary confinement.

My nephew is terrified because after the severe body beating he took, punches to the body, knee to the throat and numerous baton chokeholds. Topping it off with a beating and chokehold to sign a document stating no injuries, after they beat him and an additional chokehold and threat by Sergeant Merigold forcing him to submit to an AIDS test so they could justify beating him to a pulp, while Correction Officer Cefaloni inflicts injury to himself via biting his finger and placing blame on my nephew. Oh and they made sure not to touch his face. That's the oldest trick in the corrupt Correction Officer playbook. Take Correction Officer Cefaloni DNA immediately.

When you have the new Superintendent Griffin vocally giving the green light to physical abuse the inmates and falsify use of force and incident reports to cover their misconduct and portray inmates to look like wild animals that are guilty. There is nothing no one could do. Who believes an inmate?

My nephew was transferred to Green Haven on February 24, 2012, for good behavior. They are now trying to strip him of his right to remain in a prison that has more opportunities to fight his case. Along with stigmatizing his record so any institution he is assigned to, he will be open to mistreatment from the welcoming facility Correction Officers. I know how this works because like I said I am a retired Correction Officer and that's what officers do. They flag the documents and write things on their documents to cause them abuse from receiving Correction Officers..

My nephew comes from a family of law enforcement (Correction Officers, Police Officers, Detectives and Court Officers) He is not some wild animal that goes berserk. His record speaks for itself. He has not been in any trouble in years. He is fighting to get his sentence overturned not fighting Correction Officers to add additional time to his sentence or spend the time in solitary confinement.

Investigating my nephews incident equipped with the inside knowledge because I worked in the prison system for 20 years. I know all too well. In the 80's I worked under a Warden who ordered Correction Officers to beat down inmates and stated he will take care of the paperwork. Obviously this took place because it took them several days to submit the charges. When I personally spoke to the SHU counselor Alvin Reed, all he saw was a small ticket on my nephew's record. Why did they take so long to issue a ticket? They were getting their stories and paperwork together to make it stick.

Nevertheless, I am forwarding this document to the Inspector General, but due to my past experience with city inspector general, I do not know who is in bed with the Superintendent, Captain Cary, Lieutenant Murphy, Sergeants Merigold ,Ragloon, Mulligani or Correction Officer Cefaloni, because obviously Cefaloni has some kind of power because beating and violating inmates rights has landed him in major complaint box and he is supposed to have no inmate contact to a certain degree. He along with Correction Officer Friedman are known thought-out the institution for assaulting inmates, and getting away with it.

Therefore can you please send in a special unit immediately to fully investigate the brutal beating and torture they inflicted, on my nephew on November 29, 2014 at 9am along with the other inmates who are routinely beaten and have their rights violated by the Green Haven State Correction administration also.

I am not sure if this they were upset because my nephew was very vocal about the wrongdoing committed by the Correction Officers or this is retaliation for the memoir/novel I am writing about corruption among the New York City Correction Officers. Reporter Gary Buiso from the New York Post conducted an interview about my upcoming memoir/novel that is about to be published.

http://nypost.com/2014/08/31/sex-drug-abuse-rampant-at-rikers-retired-officer/

It is common knowledge amongst the Correction Officers at Green Haven Delamar Brown's aunt is a retired NYC Correction Officer and is writing a book about corrupt Correction Officers, Commissioners, Wardens and Captain. Therefore it makes me wonder if this out of the blue, disdain Captain Carey has for my nephew is in relation to my book because my nephew clearly stated to me he has no idea why they lied and definitely doesn't know any of the correction officers who beat him down. I also received a call that while they were knowingly violating institutional procedures and his rights a Lieutenant on that particular Saturday shift said he wanted no parts of it.

11/29/2014 at approximately 1330 hours I received a telephone call from Green Haven Correctional Facility, informing me the Correction Officers at Greenhaven Correctional Facility jumped my nephew and beat him up and to get him a lawyer. I immediately called the jail and was told to call back Monday. I received a series of call from prison inmate's family members with the same information. I called Green Haven back Monday morning to discover he was transferred to Sing Sing mental health. I called Sing Sing ext. 1220, mental health and spoke to Mike Steinbaccer at 1243 hours. He called me back an hour later and informed me my nephew was there. I asked him if he was ok and if he was beat up. He said my nephew was ok and he did not see any scars on his face but my nephew said his body was sore. At that point I knew he was beat in the body and knew they had something to hide. As a Correction Officer I observed on many occasions my colleagues doing the same thing. Beat the inmate in a way the scars are not really visible. They threaten the inmate to either refuse medical treatment or claim no injuries. Once they sign on the dotted line the officer is covered. The officer in turns writes a very damaging UOF and incident report to make sure the inmates is on the losing end. They can get anyone to write statements including other officers and inmates. It depends how afraid an officer is, of their superior officers or the inmate can get special treatment. My nephew needs medical attention and has scars but if someone doesn't get there soon they will disappear.

After they made my nephew refuse medical treatment and forcibly take an AIDS test they sent him to the Solitary Confinement area and procedure is you have to fill out a form. There were several questions and he wrote yes to two of them and a red flag went up. He had to be transferred to Sing Sing Mental health facility because he checked yes to those two questions.

Well Sergeant Merigold did not take too kindly to my nephew leaving the facility. As a result the Sergeant approached him with the four transport Correction Officers. Sergeant Merigold stated" So you want to play games. We played our game you play your game. I am sending you with four of my special officers. Oh and you will be back. I'll make this 45 minute ride a two hour ride." Delamar stated the drive threatened him all the way to Sing Sing . I think they were afraid he would blow the whistle on them. So one of the Correction Officers handed the lieutenant a note to make sure they treat him unfairly. The Lieutant asked Delamar what happened because she remembered him from

Green Haven. He told her he didn't know, he was about to come off keep lock, beat down by the officers and put in the box. She said okay and he said the Correction staff there was very nice to him. My guess is that Lieutenant worked there and got the hell out because of the corruption.

(ABUSE OF POWER -FALSIFYING DOCUMENTS)

Sergeants Ragloon and Mulligani ordered Correction Officer Ellis to falsify documents and write an infraction on Delamar Brown, placing him in a temporary solitary (keep lock) situation. The first infraction was for a lamp in his cell that she states was covered. During the hearing Delamar attempting to appeal the violation, and brought to the attention of Lieutenant Murphy who conducted the hearing, that he doesn't own a lamp. The Lieutenant Murphy stated for Delamar to "Shut the fuck up and take the loss of commissary and days on keep and get the fuck out of here. He went back to his cell and without warning was written up again for doing absolutely nothing. Female Correction Officer Ellis apologized to my nephew and said Sergeant Mulligani told her to write Delamar up again. My nephew told her not to worry about it because he understood because she was new. She falsified the document stating he cursed her out, apparently out of fear of her superior officers; she did what she was ordered to do.

As a rookie Correction Officer I was physically abused by a male Correction Officer and taunted by my colleagues thereafter. Someone needs to question and protect her from whistle blowing because she holds the key to the corruption amongst her colleagues. It was her initial bogus write up that set the pace for this paper trail conspiracy. I am quite sure once this document is submitted worldwide she will catch back lash from her superior officers and colleagues. At that point she will probably fear for her job and continue to lie or blow the lid off the corruption. If she is assured of protection she might tell the truth.

(EXCESSIVE FORCE) 11/29/2014 Approximately 0900 hrs

Female Correction Officer Dejesus was the escort officer to and from the Tier 2 hearing. Upon leaving the hearing office at 0900hrs, by building 12 H Block corridor, there were several officers awaiting his arrival. Correction Officer Cefaloni (not sure of correct spelling) led the pack. Present was Correction Officer Jamison , Sergeant Merigold ,

Female Correction Officer Howard, and 3 unidentified Caucasian male Correction Officers. Correction Officer Cefaloni stated to my nephew that he had so much to say now he got his boys there, what he was going to do. Delamar was puzzled because he was unfamiliar with Correction Officer Cefaloni. Cefaloni told him to take his hands out his pocket to fight and Delamar refused. Cefaloni and the 3 unidentified officers commenced to beating him with the baton, striking him numerous times on his legs and body, using the same baton to put him in a chokehold. Cefaloni also had his knee on Delamr's throat. They beat him for several minutes as Captain Daniel Carey observed. He ordered the hit on my nephew. I guess he wanted to make sure they were beating him to a pulp. The beating stopped and female Correction Officer Dejesus escorted him to his cell. At some point before they arrive at Delamar's cell, in close proximity to the mess hall , Correction Officer Cefaloni jumped out of nowhere, ran up behind Delamar and struck him hard in the back of the neck and leg with his baton. He put him in a chokehold with the baton, handcuffed him and hit him numerous times in the body area. Now he had to be escorted to the hospital. When he reached the hospital inside the jail, the nurse was told to leave the room. They have cameras in the hospital. They threatened him made him sign an injury report claiming no injuries.

Now I expect them to lie and state Delamar Brown started the incident to cover up their actions because this is common in this institution. They also know where to beat inmates in the blind spots in the jails where there are no cameras. Correction Officer Cefaloni went as far as either biting his own finger or getting someone else to do it to state Delamar bit him that is why they beat him. Delamar wants the authorities to check the DNA immediately. He could not understand why they physically forced him to take and AIDS test when he never fought back and they made sure to beat him in his body so no blood was present. I have worked with Correction Officers in the past that used these tactics to cover-up beat downs on prisoners. These Correction Officers know how to beat a prisoner's body and leave very little visual marks.

106

THESE ARE THE THINGS THAT MIGHT HAPPEN IF MY NEPHEW IS NOT PROTECTED

1. He might be found dead in his cell and they will claim suicide

2. The Correction Officer pay another inmate to physically injure kill or my nephew while he is in the box yard, before they manage to get the handcuffs off.

3. The food sent to him through the mess hall has poison and they slowly kill him or make him violently sick.

4. A weapon or drugs is planted in his cell

5. False allegation that he attacked an officer or staff member so they beat him up again.

6. Slipped in the shower and hit his head and is in a coma.

7. They will transfer him far away before he has a chance to fight his appeal. Or force him to sign a document he doesn't want him to appeal this new bogus violation.

8. DEATH OR COMA

Any possible scenario you can think of I am expecting to happen. It is know that Captain Cary doesn't give a damn. He's afraid of nothing and will be angry I am submitting this report to every agency possible. There will be consequences for beating up my nephew for nothing or because I am writing a book about corrupt Correction Officers. I will be to the facility to visit my nephew every week to ensure he is safe. My nephew is appealing his new charges and will be vindicated if an investigation is conducted by an outside agency.

I expect the Correction Officers to give me a hard time under his orders, or make false allegations against me to possibly prevent me from visiting my nephew. Or tamper with my car in the parking lot while I am visiting him, to cause me to have an accident. Yes I know it's a long stretch, but judging on the beat down and tactics they used against my nephew, especially the officer biting his own finger , claiming my nephew did it. I know there is nothing they wouldn't do.

In summation the goons squad, Superintendent, Captain Daniel Cary and Sergeant Merigold, Correction Officer Cefaloni and Correction Officer Friedman are patrolling the jail inflict deadly physical force on inmates. They give excellent honest Correction Officers and higher ups a bad name. They know how to falsify documents and cover-up wrongdoings.

Captain Daniel Cary on the other hand is the main culprit at Green Haven Correctional facility. He orchestrates evildoings at the jail. I don't know if it's because he is a racist or a sick individual. He has my nephew on his personal hit list and they said he will not stop until he makes his life a living hell. What else can he do after this ordeal he was placed under? KILL HIM and wait for the grand jury to not indict him. It is common knowledge every Correction Officer, inmate, and probably some of his subordinates in Green Haven are petrified of Captain Cary. They say once you get on that bad side he will make your life a living hell and he knows his paper work and can get out of anything. So he doesn't give a damn who makes complaints. He does exactly what he wants to do. Who the hell does he think he is? This is abuse of power to the highest degree. The jail is afraid of Captain Daniel Cary. This one individual has control of the fate of anyone in that jail He has hid behind his tenure, paperwork, white shirt and higher up connections. There are so many inmates who have been injured in this facility and the public knows nothing about. One guy's legs and arms were broken over the summer. They covered that up. There are so many complaints against Correction Officer Cefaloni I would like to know how he has remained in that building long enough to brutally beat my nephew. Please pull this Cefaloni's UOF record and I want answers as to how he managed to have physical contact with my nephew. I do not want to hear the perjury edition. I am going to contact each and every agency until I make sure my nephew is taken out of harms way because this is foul. I am also going to file a lawsuit against Green Haven for falsifying documents and the beatings and chokeholds they performed on my nephew. They purposely concocted this scenario to take him out of a decent jail where he is close to home, and his family can visit. To place him in a disciplinary institution way up in the mountains whereas it is difficult for his family and lawyer to reach him. I've seen this corruption too many times and I will not sit back and let it happen to anyone else. Inspector General needs to investigate this institution and eliminate the physical abuse. They should plant Correction Officers and inmates. The American Civil Liberties Union needs to investigate the complaints. There are entirely too many inmates beaten excessively, with broken limbs and their rights violated. There is still Correction Officers distributing drugs at that facility. Once these inmates are placed in Solitary confinement the Correction Officers are putting feces and urine in their food so they cannot eat, or just plain ole not feeding them. Something needs to be done. I have a list of people below I am forwarding this document to. I will definitely reach out to 100's more.

Respectfully Submitted

Robin K Miller

CC: President Barack Obama,Vice President Biden,

First Lady Michelle Obama,Dr. Jill Biden,

US Attorney Preet Bharara,Governor Andrew Cuomo

NYS Inspector General Catherine Leahy Scott

Acting Commissioner Anthony J. Annucci,

Deputy Commissioner for Correctional Facilities Joseph Bellnier

New York Civil Liberties Union Donna Lieberman,Vanita Gupta, the Center for Justice ,Superintendent Griffin Green Haven Correctional Facility ,New York Post Gary Buiso , Artyom Matusov ,Al Sharpton

December 11, 2014

Dear President Barack Obama,

My name is Robin K Miller. I am a retired New York City Correction Officer. I faxed you a document on December 5, 2014 (see attached) regarding the New York State Correction Officers at Green Haven Correctional Facility in Stormville New York 12582. They almost murdered my nephew Delamar Brown with baton choke holds and over 100 baton blows to the body. I do not want another Eric Garner situation, and wrongfully placed him in solitary confinement, violating his civil rights, to cover their actions. My nephew did not know why he was singled out or who these Correction Officers were. He has no past history with these officers and they are the official goon squad of the jail. Every jail has a goon squad. I know firsthand. Therefore I am assuming it is because of the memoirs I am writing regarding corruption at Rikers Island in the New York City. An article was written by the New York Post and I know it angered many correction officers (city & state). http://nypost.com/2014/08/31/sex-drug-abuse-rampant-at-rikers-retired-officer/

The Correction Officers and administration have officially committed a criminal act by covering up the incident by falsifying business records and offering a false instrument for filing, both felonies, and other misdemeanors, including official misconduct .

The proof is in the document (violation ticket) he received on December 4, 2014. Correction Officer Cefaloni is the only party named in the violation. He falsified the official document by stating he alone assaulted my nephew. Captain Cary, Sergeant Merigold was present during the attempted murder on my nephew. They are listed nowhere in the report. All of the correction staff listed in my letter is not listed in the report as well. That is a crime and punishable by law. Correction Officer Cefaloni is falsifying legal documents and the administration allowed him to submit it.

I went to visit my nephew on 12/4/2014 at GreenHaven Correctional Facility and he gave me a detailed statement about the horrific incident on 11/29/14. He was not served his violation ticket as of 12/4/2014 prior to or during visiting hours. They had no idea my nephew was giving me a detailed statement and I was going to document it. After the visit with my nephew ended, my nephew was escorted back to his cell and received his fraudulent violation/ticket. We had no further contact until I returned on 12/10/2014.

Superintendent Griffin, Correction Officer Cefaloni, Captain Cary , Sergeant Merigold had no idea I was submitting a report to Attorney General Eric Holder and forwarded it to you and various agencies. They probably figured they would serve my nephew with bogus charges and the process would be cut and dry. Judging on their initial behavior, it is safe to assume, they were probably going to physically force him to sign and accept the charges. Once he was convicted on those bogus charges he would be sent to the major solitary confinement jail and his life would be a living hell, once assault on officer is on his record. That label would follow him his entire time in any facility he is incarcerated in, until I can get his sentence overturned.

When I returned on 12/10/2014, I learned there was a cover-up in progress and also learned Inspector General still had not interviewed my nephew. I spoke directly to State Inspector General James Cross on 12/5/2014 at approximately 1300 hours. He gave me his direct email address and I also forwarded him a copy of the letter to James Cross james.cross@doccs.ny.gov.

I am respectfully requesting you send the justice department to the jail to investigate this matter. The inspector general is obviously in bed with the administration and failed to act.

Inspector General James Cross needs to be fully investigated. How many complaints has he received concerning wrongdoing? How many investigation has he conducted with enough evidence confirming criminal acts by the correction officers, that were unfounded by him? I called him and told him the correction officers at Greenhaven Correctional facility attempted murder on my nephew and he tells me to hold on and returns to the phone to tell me my nephew assaulted the officers. I briefly explained what happened and also expressed my distrust in inspector general.

My nephew has been singled out, beaten and wrongfully placed in solitary confinement. Everyday he sits in solitary confinement; it is a violation of his civil rights. It is the state's responsibility to ensure this type of

111

ordeal is addressed, especially after it is brought to their attention. He should be removed from solitary confinement immediately.

Everyday those Correction Officers and the administration are not punished for their illegal actions are a miscarriage of justice. I contacted you in 2005, before your presidency, while my nephew was on trial because his civil rights were being violated by the judge and district attorney (delamarbrown.com). You can view the documents there. I never received a response. I hope you can look into this matter now because I am still in fear for his safety and it wouldn't surprise me if they somehow take the ticket they falsified and discard. They are continuing to violate him through the hearing process. He is appealing the charges. All the Correction Officers involved in the incident need to be brought up on criminal and institutional charges, If you had a son constantly wronged by the criminal justice system. Would you sit back and do absolutely nothing. I will fight this matter and not rest until my nephew is removed from solitary confinement status and those superior officers and correction officers are dealt with properly.

Respectfully Submitted

Robin K Miller

CC;Vice President Biden

First Lady Michelle Obama

Dr. Jill Biden

Norman Siegel

US Attorney Preet Bharara

Governor Andrew Cuomo

NYS Inspector General Catherine Leahy Scott

Acting Commissioner Anthony J. Annucci

Deputy Commissioner for Correctional Facilities Joseph Bellnier

Artyom Matusov

Prison Legal Services - James Bogin

December 26, 2014

Re: Green Haven Correction Officers Attempt Murder on Delamar Brown

To Attorney General Eric Holder,

My name is Robin K. Miller. I am a retired New York City Correction Officer. This document is regarding the Delamar Brown case in GreenHaven Correctional facility, in Stormville New York. This is an update regarding the wrongdoing that continues at this facility among the administration.

I received some disturbing news today. It appears that there is a major cover-up surrounding the facts of the case. They are not allowing his witness to come forth and speak at the hearing, after repeatedly informing the Correction Officers they want to testify.

I am privy to inside information that the administration convinced a nurse, to alter the original documents to make it appear she did in fact exam my nephew. I also learned they threw away the photos that display his injuries to his body. You can clearly see on the photos his leg is twice the size it should be. I sure hope that is not true because that is against the law. The nurse needs her license revoked and I will see to it she is investigated and request all of her past cases pulled for review. How many times did she falsify documents to justify their corrupt and criminal actions.

However judging from their actions of brutally beating my nephew, its not hard to believe they are trying to cover their tracks. I also learned that Correction Officer Cefaloni is filing more false reports regarding the incident on the extensive report. How many times did they also the date to reflect it was written on the actual date of occurrence? When in all actuality it was written after they viewed the documents I sent to you Attorney General Holder on November 5 & 6.

They are trying to railroad my nephew Delamar Brown after they brutally beat him. I sent all of these documents to The State Correction Commissioner and Inspector General and nothing has been done. I am respectfully requesting the justice department investigate Greenhaven Correctional facility. As you recall, this is the facility that was recently in the news for contraband. There is a whole lot more going on here. They changed the administration but not the mindset.

I also would like the justice department to investigate the SHU counselor Alvin Reed. He is in bed with the administration and refusing to properly counsel and address my nephews concerns. He told me he is overworked and I should suggest they hire more counselors. He has given me false information and is rude and disrespectful to my nephew. He is not supposed to take sides. He is just supposed to counsel. I think he has been at this command too long and needs to be re-trained and transferred. He brags about 17 years on the job but is refusing to properly do his job. There are numerous complaints from every inmate under his supervision and their family members. It would not surprise me if a document is not included by him, in this fraudulent case that reflects my nephew's willingness to cooperate. It would not surprise me if he does not paint my nephew as a wild animal to remain in the good graces of the administration at Greenhaven Correctional facility. All of the inmates under his supervision need to be interviewed. There will be a class action suit against Counselor Reed by the inmates and their families.

If the information I received is indeed true about the administration altering legal documents regarding my nephew Delamar Brown's case. They need to be prosecuted and I will see to it they are prosecuted. I will force the staff that is leaking the information to me to come forth or they will be prosecuted too. Correction Officer Cefaloni and his cronies crossed the line when they used excessive force and denied him medical attention. Falsifying legal documents is a crime and every Correction Officer knows that. Please send the justice department to oversee this process. My nephew is not going to get a fair hearing. There will be altered documents, lost photos of injuries and witnesses denied access to testify. Once this hearing is conducted and these fraudulent documents are included the crime has officially be committed.

Respectfully Submitted,

Robin K Miller

CC: President Barack Obama

Vice President Biden

Acting Commissioner Anthony J. Annucci

Attorney Norman Siegel

US Attorney Preet Bharara

Governor Andrew Cuomo

NYS Inspector General Catherine Leahy Scott

Deputy Commissioner for Correctional Facilities Joseph Bellnier

Prison Legal Services- James Bogin

New York Civil Liberties Union Donna Lieberman

Vanita Gupta, the Center for Justice

Superintendent Griffin Green Haven Correctional Facility

January 9, 2015

Dear Attorney General Eric Holder.

My name is Robin K Miller. I am a retired New York City Correction Officer. This document is regarding my nephew Delamar Brown (case ID# 2942366). I would like to thank you for viewing the documents and assigning the case to someone in your bureau. I am aware this case is newly assigned.

A copy of a document was just forwarded to me. This document was written by inmate Shamel Burrough 93A5731, who is currently housed in Greenhaven Correctional facility. On November 29, 2014 he wrote a letter (see attached) to Superintendent Griffin regarding the use of deadly physical force against my nephew, Delamar Brown 06B2999. He was also a witness and testified at the hearing for my nephew. Several days later, he was escorted to the hearing room again without the knowledge of my nephew, and some form of intimidation tactics were used by the correction staff to get Shamel Burrough 93A5731 to change his testimony.

I have several concerns regarding the tactics that are being instituted at the GreeenHaven Correctional Facility by the Correction Officers. My major concern besides the deadly physical force used on my nephew, is the Correction Officers are going to physical abuse or set up inmate via (planting weapons, drugs, falsifying documents or strong arming him into changing his testimony because it is damaging. I have a suspicion that they are going to try everything in their power to try to discredit Shamel Burrough and get him shipped out of the building.

As I viewed the letter he wrote to Superintendent Griffin immediately following the assault on my nephew is damaging because it coincides with what my nephew stated happened. Shamel Burrough 93A5731 did not have physical or verbal contact with my nephew before, during or after the incident. It is obvious to me this type of behavior is rampant and accepted by the superior officers in Greenhaven Correctional Facility. The Correction Officers have been physically abusing the inmates without consequences for a very long time.

I have in my possession a copy of all the documents submitted by and according to Correction Officer Cefaloni's Use of Force report, there were 40–50 inmates in the hallways. He never mentioned the gang of Correction Officer awaiting Delamar Brown, armed with their baton's to jump Delamar . Why? I am quite sure the 40-50 inmates can confirm Delamar was jumped by the Correction Officers. I received several calls to my home, from family members of these inmates stating the Correction Officers jumped my nephew. I called the jail immediately.

Delamar was heard by inmate Shamel Burrough repeatedly stating "WHAT DID I SAY, WHAT DID I SAY?   YOUR GONNA JUMP ME?) Why would Shamel Burrough write that? He wrote that because his statement is accurate and Superintendent Griffin knows it.

Correction Officer E. Dejesus was escorting Delamar Brown into an ambush. She was fully aware they were going to beat him down. If he was talking while she was escorting him, she would have heard the first words out of his mouth and told him to stop talking. She is covering up the incident and needs to be fired. If you read her report, it is the same exact report that Correction Officer Cefaloni wrote. I worked as a Correction Officer for 20 years before I retired and know how this is done. Everyone sits down together and writes the same report.

Delamar Brown refused medical treatment, even though several inmates witnessed him being unable to walk to the clinic. However he agreed to take an HIV/AIDS test. No they strong armed him into refusing medical treatment, and after that beating he was subjected to, Delamar was petrified. It's obvious they threatened another baton beating because, why would he refuse medical treatment for himself and submits to medical treatment so Correction Officer Cefaloni could build a bogus case, to justify him and his fellow officers use of deadly physical force. Delamar sustained injuries and without seeing a doctor, taking x-rays and MRI's that strengths the reports submitted by Correction Officer Cefaloni. He needs to be arrested and fired. This is not his first incident. Delamar is requesting the footage of area for the entire morning this incident. The photos of Correction Officer Cefaloni bitten hand are bogus. Not only does it not prove to be his hand. It could be someone else's hand.

I suspect at this time the staff is going to approach some of the inmate's present during the assault on Delamar and either threatens them into writing a false document to confirm the correction officers' story. Or threaten them into not testifying. There are several inmates that want to testify but are afraid because they know the Correction Officers always get away with beating up prisoner. It's a known fact if an officer doesn't like you they will beat you up and say you assaulted them.

I find it odd that hearings and incidents occur primarily on the weekends when Superintendents are not present. The same way they escorted Delamar to a hearing early Saturday morning on November 29, 2014, and Shamel Burrough on a Saturday to persuade him to change his testimony. I suspect if they haven't already. They will call inmate Shamel Burrough back to the hearing room this weekend g

This facility is corrupt. The drug bust in August 2014 was just the tip of the iceberg. As I conduct my own investigation I have learned this jail is known for drug smuggling and unnecessary abuse on inmates.

I am respectfully requesting someone interview Shamel Burrough and my nephew immediately. He is continuously being penalized for something he did not do. Every day in SHU violates his constitutional rights.

Counselor Alvin Reed is refusing to counsel him. I guess this is part of the plan to paint Delamar as an animal that attacks Correction Officer. You look at his record since he has been incarcerated. That is not his pedigree. They are also feeding him dog slop and someone from OSHA or one of those agencies need to investigate the food being served to the inmates in SHU. I guarantee you it differs from the norm. The inmates in SHU are starving while they are being feed gravy and noodles disguised as a gourmet meal. They might as well feed them bread and water. I know its being done deliberately. The inmates are starving. Why? No I do not expect him to be catered to or gourmet meals. However torture is not on the menu either.

If there was any doubt in my mind that Delamar was responsible in any form or fashion. I would not pursue this matter. I have been conducting my own investigation and the information and activities I am discovering is mind-boggling. That fact that inspector general hasn't responded to my letters faxed and certified mail is familiar. I experienced this same type of response when I reported wrongdoing as a city correction officer.

I suspect this is in retaliation because I am penning my memoirs about corrupt correction officers. My nephew has had no problems with Correction Officers ever and out of the blue he is being targeted. The only thing they didn't take into account was his aunt Robin K Miller stepping forth to correct this wrongdoing and I will not stop until justice is served. I will not go away and expect them to target me soon.

http://nypost.com/2014/08/31/sex-drug-abuse-rampant-at-rikers-retired-officer/

Respectfully Submitted

Robin K Miller

CC:

President Obama

Vice President Biden

Attorney Norman Siegel

Delamar Brown

US Attorney Preet Bharara

United States Attorney's Office

Governor Andrew Cuomo

NYS Inspector General Catherine Leahy Scott

Acting Commissioner Anthony J. Annucci

Deputy Commissioner for Correctional Facilities Joseph Bellnier

New York Post Gary Buiso

Superintendent Griffin Green Haven Correctional Facility

Troop K Commander Senior Investigator Hettwer

Counselor Alvin Reed

To: Mr. Superintendent
From: Shamel Burroughs #93A5731
Date: 11-29-14

Dear Sir

I'm writing you concerning your officers
behavior. it's getting really frustrated with our present living
condition where we have to live under the constant threat
of abuse and assault. on the above date I witness officers
verbally abuse Inmate Brown E-256. for no reason at
all. officer DeJesus was escorting Inmate Brown from a
tier hearing when he was apptoched by the officer
working outside the H-Block Bubble. Supposely Inmate Brown
was to supposely had said something to this officer previously
because the inmate kept on asking "What did I say". the
officer realized that it was around 20 to 35 Inmates
in the Hall at that time & told us to past by. upon us
pasting I heard Inmate Brown state "your gonna jump
on me". that's when I heard some scraping sound. officer
J. Goehl, officer Erick was there along with officer DeJesus
officer DeJesus could've avioded this by simply doing her
Job by escorting him to the hearing and back to his
cell. But being that it's no consequences for these
officers action they continue to assault & abuse people.
This type of behavior is unacceptable and would no
longer be accepted. this epidemic that you have here
in this facility where officers assault & abuse people

daily is condoned with a blind eye. Then you &
your administration justify these assaults with fictitious
assault on staff when in fact the Inmate is the
one who recieved all the injuries. The actions of
these officers is one of evil minded & oppressive
behavior. When you walk around with a stick out
trying to intimidate & abuse people is the opposite
of which you was hired for. the object of the
job is care custody & control. Not use of force
when you feel like it but when it's needed.

January 16, 2015

Dear Federal Bureau of Investigations,

This document is regarding my nephew Delamar Brown 06B2999, Green Haven Correctional Facility, and our conversation yesterday, concerning the corruption, cover-up and Delamar's need for medical attention. I want to thank you for at least viewing my documents and listening to me.

As a New York City Correction Officer, I am familiar with Correction Officers beating up inmates for no reason, other than egos. After they beat the inmates up, they make them refuse medical attention so the injuries are not documented to prove an assault occurred. They used to beat the inmate solely on his body and eventually the bruises will go away.

Delamar stated photos were taken that day and can show his right leg is twice the size of his left leg. It would not surprise me if the photos are now missing.

Every week I visit him, he is complaining. His right hand, arm and leg are numb, his right eye was twitching uncontrollable during the entire visit on 1-14-2015, and he has blurred vision and constant headaches. There is a great possibility he has nerve damage on the right side of his body. He needs to go to an outside hospital and they are refusing him medical attention. On page 2 (see attached) of the Unusual Incident Report Nurse T Daly noted no injuries. Nurse T Daly is in cohorts with the administration and needs to be fired immediately.

I wanted to give you some updated information and its imperative someone speaks to Delamar and his witnesses from the hearing. As a matter of fact the FBI needs to find the 40 or 50 inmates that Correction Officer Cefaloni wrote in his report (see attached) to Superintendent Griffin dated 11/29/2014. The 40-50 inmates were going to religious services that morning. Why they were not questioned is a mystery to me?

The concerns I am having right now is no matter how much evidence and testimony that favors Delamar. He will lose the hearing because Deputy Superintendent Collado is conducting a kangaroo court hearing.

Delamar had faith in her that she was being fair. She is playing the good cop bad cop role. These inmates had no verbal or physical contact with Delamar during or after the incident

Case and point: She is trying to discredit Delamar's witnesses and weaken his case. If you listen to the tapes at the hearings you can clearly hear she is not impartial. She is siding with Correction Officer Cefaloni, even if it means violating Delamar's rights and breaking the law.

For starters when the Correction Officer Jamison testified, the first thing she did was slide the previous reports written by Officer Cefaloni across the desk to Correction Officer Jamison and told him to refresh his memory before he speaks. Delamar was disturbed and told her that was unfair. Unbeknownst to Deputy Superintendent Collado Correction Officer Jamison's told the truth and his story coincides with Delamar's Shamel Burroughs, Carlos Garcia 89T1556, and his other witnesses. He stated Correction Officer Cefaloni was arguing and also placed four or more Correction Officers present at the incident prior to the assault. Correction Officer Cefaloni report does not mention any other Correction Officers at the scene. Why? It's because he falsified a legal document .

Deputy Superintendent's Collado's response to Delamar when he mentioned he has all this testimony in his favor, including Correction Officer Jamison's testimony was: inmate Shamel Burroughs is lying because Superintendent Griffin never received a letter. Shamel Burroughs wrote the letter (see attached) immediately after the incident and placed it in the institutional mail box. It's not like he can walk to Superintendent Griffin's office door and say while you were enjoying your day off, Saturday 11/29/2014, your officer's jumped Delamar Brown.

Also I recently learned inmate Peter Anekwe 99A2717 approached Sergeant Cousins before the incident went into full effect and told him to get down to the corridor because they were going to do something to inmate Brown. Whoever this Sergeant Cousins is, he ignored him and 10 minutes there was an alarm. Peter Anekwe, also sent a letter to Superintendent Griffin. I informed Delamar about Peter's letter and told him to call him as a witness, and he said Deputy Superintendent Collado said he could not have anymore witnesses, it would be redundant. She is not interested in getting to the truth. She is only interested in clearing Correction Officer Cefaloni.

I also learned, after Carlos Garcia testified, they packed him up and moved him from his cell, to another part of the jail. I fear they did something to him and someone needs to go and speak to him. They are either going to set him up, make him change his story or have him beat up by another inmate. That is witness tampering

I warned Delamar not to be fooled by Collado because she works for Superintendent Griffin and there is no way she is going to find guilt in Correction Officer Cefaloni because Superintendent Griffin could be cited for failure to supervise. Collado states Superintendent Griffin never received the mail. If that is accurate, then an investigation needs to be conducted as to why someone tampered with the mail and he never received inmate Shamel Burroughs or Peter Anekwe's letter. These inmates know the consequences of coming forth. They have a lot to lose by testifying because they are placed on a hit list. There is no reason why they would lie and risk being subjected to further abuse from the correction staff and transferred into the mountains. When they cam remain close to home and their families can visit them.

Someone needs to review Correction Officer Jamison's testimony, but I would not be surprised if somehow they were able to re-record his testimony, because they will stop at nothing to cover this up.

I am starting to put all of this together and I warned Attorney General Holder in my first letter that the high ranking officers at Greenhaven Correctional Facility are highly connected. It's obvious because I wrote to the NYS Inspector General Catherine Leahy Scott, Acting Commissioner Anthony J. Annucci and Deputy Commissioner for Correctional Facilities Joseph Bellnier and no one has interviewed Delamar as of yet and his injuries are not going away. He needs an MRI and X-RAYS taken. He was assaulted by state employees, not inmates. They need to foot the bill. Acting Commissioner Anthony J. Annucci and Captain Cary are buddies; there are pictures of them together. Captain Cary received an award. That is why no one from the Commissioner's office has responded. Captain Cary was present during the gang assault on Delamar. Why didn't he submit a report?

It's obvious they are all working from the same playbook. Deputy Superintendent Collado needs to be investigated and demoted. She doesn't deserve her position. She is in charge of the hearings and is not following the guidelines, instituting cruel punishment that doesn't coincide with institutional violations. She is finding inmates guilty of violations they didn't commit or instituting them with harsh penalties

They say she is new and doesn't know what she is doing. It's either that, she is freelancing attempting to make a good impression on her boss, or under strict orders to crucify all inmates at hearings. She is violating the policies set forth by Albany and costing the taxpayers money when these inmates sue and win on an appeal. . How many hearing penalties were overturned?

I am respectfully requesting someone look at all of her decisions she has made at her kangaroo court, in just the last month, better yet since she has taken over new position at Green Haven Correctional Facility and demote her. It's in black and white.

Everyone is in cohorts with this cover-up, beginning with his Counselor Alvin Reed. He is refusing to counsel Delamar because he knows Delamar will complain about his injuries and he will have to document it. He should be fired because he is not counseling the inmates and giving false information to inmates and their families. He needs to be investigated; all his files need to be confiscated. He is working hand in hand with the administration and whatever he writes can hold weight.

Correction Officer Cefaloni clearly lied on his reports and needs to be criminally charged. I guarantee you if you pull his Use of Force record you will discover he is a loose cannon and this is not his first time using excessive force. He needs to be given a polygraph test about the incident. Why the other Correction Officer was's who jumped Delamar, excluded from the reports? Correction Officer Trumbull stated he didn't see anything; meanwhile he was in close proximity of the incident. He doesn't want to get involved.

Correction Officers smuggling drugs into the facility is not the only problem and it is probably still going on. Excessive use of force is and has been rampant throughout the years. Green Haven is a privileged jail and inmates transfer there for good behavior. They are targeted by overzealous egotistical Correction Officers. They are using deadly physical force, making them refuse medical treatment, falsifying reports and transferred out scarred for their duration in jail. It will be difficult in any jail when their floor card is flagged with assault on officer stamped in red. I know the playbook.

From what I understand this is one of the worst jails regarding assaults on inmates. They have a highly protected goon squad, ask Sergeant Merigold.

Also grant Correction Officer Dejesus and Trumbull immunity and make them tell the truth under the FBI interrogation lights. As a matter of fact question all the Correction Officer's on duty 11/29/2014 (day shift) who were in close proximity of the incident. I guarantee you, if they are protected by the FBI for the duration of their career, they will tell you exactly what is going on in the jail. Not just the abuse but the drugs, weapons and abuse of power. Don't take my word for it. Look over all of the reports, listen to the testimonies, pull the footage from the jails displaying Delamar unable to properly walk to the clinic. Look at Correction Officer Cefaloni's hands. Did he have on any protective hand gear? If so how did Delamar bite him? Did he get a tetanus shot for the bite to his finger? No he went to his regular doctor the next day. So what does he do now, go to his doctor and tell him to write he gave him a tetanus shot and date it for 11/30/2014. Look at the bogus photos submitted. Which Correction Officers hand is in the pictures? There is no proof that it is Correction Officer's Cefaloni's hand. The bottom line is he falsified documents and the administration is covering up.

I have been down this road fighting the criminal justice system. I am disheartened by the manner in which my nephew Delamar Brown has been wrongfully convicted and constantly railroaded by the very system I gave my life to. His purpose for transferring to Green Haven was to work on his case and get his sentence overturned. I am used to agencies and people turning their backs on me and Delamar, but it makes me fight harder. I guarantee you if no one takes immediate action, one of these inmates are going to be killed by the Correction Officers in Green Haven and blood will be on the hands of the New York State Department of Corrections. These people aren't worried. They know in the past they have gotten away with it. There is a difference now. I will continue to fight until justice is served. I deliberately omitted your name because it appears that once I reveal names, the higher ups make phone calls and the person disappears. Inspector General still hasn't responded.

Respectfully Submitted,

Robin K Miller

CC:

President Barack Obama

Attorney General Eric Holder

Acting Commissioner Anthony J. Annucci

Attorney Norman Siegel

Governor Andrew Cuomo

NYS Inspector General Catherine Leahy Scott

Superintendent Griffin

State Police Investigator Kim Hettwer

Counselor Alvin Reed

Deputy Superintendent Collado

Delamar Brown

As you can see I wrote to any and everyone and only three people responded, Civil Rights Attorney Norman Siegel, the Justice Department and Inspector General, in that order. The Justice Department did not come back with favorable results. The Inspector General division that handled the case is definitely in bed with Greenhaven Correctional Facility. They make you think they are helping , but they really batting for the other team. As far as I am concerned inspector general is full of shit, because these correction officers beat the shit out of my nephew and they should have been arrested. They have to prove me otherwise.

Norman Siegel is the only one who cared enough. God Bless him and everything he stands for. He is extremely busy and took the time out of his busy schedule, to listen to me, and go to see my nephew. I felt honored to be in his presence. I will leave it at that. You will see what is in store in the near future. It ain't over until the fat lady sings.

It is a sad that the government condones this daily abuse being instituted by the correction officers in Greenhaven Correctional Facility. What other conclusion can you come up with, when I write a letter to all of those people. I am a retired New York City Correction Officer. I kept their slaves locked up and out of harms way, did their dirty work and no one investigates, until two months later.

Well the outcome, was what was expected, he was found guilty of assaulting the correction officer and sentenced to one year in solitary confinement: Southport Correctional Facility aka; BIG BOX

I know you are probably saying why fight if no one is listening or going to help. My letters might have prevented them from killing him and I did get Norman Siegel's attention. It is also inspiring me prompting to begin a bigger mission, like putting an end to this abuse, which is highly accepted within the compounds of the walls of Greenhaven Correctional Facility.

To hear my nephew Delamar say from the very beginning that no one wins in the box, they have to fight and win in an appeal is a bunch of old slavery day bunch of bullshit! The inmates know it is a kangaroo court and will be found guilty even though they are totally innocent. It is time to change that. He transferred to this jail to be close to home and work on his case to get his sentenced overturned.

Not to have his civil rights violated. This has to stop and it will stop. As long as no one in Albany fixes this wrongdoing against my nephew and similar cases I will continue to make a whole lot of noise. If these state inmates are not doing anything, leave them alone.

After I filed complaints and Delamar was transferred to Southport Correctional facility to begin solitary confinement. I was subjected to numerous ion drug scans as retaliation for whistle blowing.

Please read the letters below. Keep in mind. This is how they treat their own.

June 16, 2015

Dear Attorney General Loretta E Lynch,

My name is Robin Kay Miller. I am a retired New York City Correction Officer. I am respectfully submitting this official document as my formal complaint regarding my safety and security that are being compromised by the administration and correction officers at New York State Southport Correction Facility. Their retaliatory actions fall under the confines of whistle blowing and retaliation. Their actions are due to the actions of because my previous complaints filed against the Superintendent Griffin, Captain Daniel Cary and employees at New York State Greenhaven Correctional Facility from November 29, 2014-January 9, 2015. My integrity is being demeaned and my nephew Delamar Brown's 06B2999 rights are being violated. I suspect this is some form of payback by the administration at GreenHaven Correctional Facility . They are attempting to silence me and place me or my nephew in the position to revoke his visits

I was instructed to respectfully submit this formal document to you directly Attorney General Loretta Lynch and forward this document to Delamar's case ID# 2942366 folder with the Justice Department. Due to the recent turn of events, it is imperative that I document my suspicions because of my status as a retired New York City Correction Officer and my reputation is on the line, and I will not allow retaliatory acts to discredit my stance on brutality and abuse that was inflicted on my nephew Delamar Brown by the Correction Officers at Greenhaven Correctional Facility. I am not a civilian. I retired with an impeccable record and peace officer status. I will not be subjected to ridicule or revenge plotting and should be covered under the whistle blowing laws. The justice department needs to further investigate and monitor this ordeal

To make it brief : On November 29, 2014 Delamar Brown 06B2999 was brutally beaten with batons and placed in chokeholds by New York State Greenhaven Correction Officer Cefaloni and several of his cronies. After receiving several calls to my home that my nephew Delamar was jumped by the correction officers, I went to visit him on December 4, 2014, approximately 6 days after the incident.

Delamar didn't have to tell me what happened. I could clearly see excessive force was implemented. I just had to investigate and find out why? My nephew was walking as though he was a handicapped person. Delamar is not a fearful person, nor is he a snitch. The entire visit reeked of fear, with him constantly looking around from him and stating he wanted to get out of that building and he wanted me to contact every agency. I asked him if he saw a doctor at the facility. He informed me he was threatened with more bloody bodily harm and chokeholds if he didn't refuse medical attention.

(See attached "Attorney General Eric Holder" December 5 & 6)

During his visit I jotted down a written statement from Delamar. I initially thought it was because I am writing my memoirs about corruption in New York City Correction. I had a two-page spread in the New York Post newspaper and Delamar had it taped on his cell wall. (See article below) However through my own investigation I learned this is common practice at Greenhaven whereas they at random call them nigger, coon, provoke and beat inmates and from what I am hearing nothing has changed. It's business as usual. Prejudice and abuse is relevant in Greenhaven Correctional Facility.

On December 5, 2014 I began contacting every agency imaginable and that angered every one in Greenhaven Correctional Facility. Primarily: Superintendent Thomas Griffin and Captain Daniel Cary. I visited Delamar every week he was in Greenhaven because I was fearful they would kill him. Every visit I attended all the superior officers were present. They were forced to respond to my allegations and it's obvious they made every effort to cover it up utilizing the old correction officer's playbook

When New York State Inspector General is compelled to tell my nephew they are aware of his beatings and the numerous beating in the building but will lose his hearing before the hearing was completed, is cause for red flags. The Inspector General was correct Delamar was found guilty because the jail administration controls the hearings.

Delamar filed his appeal and of course he lost because the Acting Commissioner Anthony J Annucci makes the final decision during the appeal process. He didn't look at the facts or didn't view it at all.

I observed pictures of him presenting an award to Captain Daniel Cary. Therefore why would the Acting Commissioner Annucci remain impartial when making his appeal decision, when he is cohorts with Captain Daniel Cary? They knew this when I started filing complaints and they now have a score to settle with me.

Once Delamar was transferred to Southport Correctional Facility, the motion for payback ensued.

I cannot confirm if Superintendent Thomas Griffin and Superintendent Patrick Griffin are related but if that is factual, Patrick Griffin was the superior officer at Southport Correctional Facility and is just a phone call away from a favor. That's how the Correction Department machine works. I know all to well. I worked for the correction department for 20 years.

My due diligence to seek justice as well as penning my memoirs exposing the corrupted behavior of my colleagues is a recipe for disaster.http:// nypost.com/2014/08/31/sex-drug-abuse-rampant-at-rikers-retired-officer/

I firmly believe my nephew and I now have a bull's-eye on our backs with Southport Correctional Facility and I will not sit back and allow them to get away with it. If wrongdoing has occurred to my family member I have every right to report it. I will not be silenced. Delamar wants me to leave it alone and just focus on his case to get him home. My Peace Officer Status will not allow that.

As a Correction Officer, I am familiar with the flagging of an inmate's institutional folder. It will reflect what the preceding facility wants the receiving facility to adhere. The transporting officer will verbally relay the dirty information to the receiving room officers at the new facility.

That will determine what kind of treatment an inmate will get at that facility. Delamar is now branded "ASSAULTS CORRECTION OFFICERS" and that in itself is a death sentence in any jail. The aftermath is detrimental to his well being and any family member that visits him. That is dangerous and a sick thing for a law enforcement regime to do to anyone and it is common practice at Greenhaven Correctional facility. I am now privy to that information.

Delamar has been incarcerated for 10 years he was involved in one situation an erroneous urinal analysis in Great Meadows Correctional Facility. I contacted Inspector General to report the Correction Officer taking money from inmates to switch urine. Delamar was very upset and refused to communicate with me on any level.

Years later a family member confided in me, the consequences my nephew suffered because of my whistle blowing. Great Meadows correction officers damaged his clothing by pouring baby oil and ink on them. He was mentally tortured and starved at Southport Correctional Facility when he arrived to commence serving 6 months in the box for dirty urine and he was drug free.

Delamar has since learned the code of silence as many inmates do in jail. They are rightfully conditioned to believe the Correction Officers can do what they want and get away with it. His folder is permanently flagged with a positive for drugs. Therefore Delamar put his best foot forward and stayed out of the realm of the systematic brutality machine until Correction Officer Cefaloni and his cronies decided he wanted to treat my nephew like a slave and beat him viciously and force his superior officers to cover it up and call on favors because it's a direct reflection of their supervision.

 I was all set to cease any further actions until they decided to single me out for the "Substance Detection/Ion Scan" on June 7, 2015 prior to my visit. I am familiar with the machine and the process. As a retired Correction Officer I do not expect any special treatment and do not have any ill feelings towards the Correction Officers at Southport Correctional Facility. Obviously they have some towards me. I did not have a problem with submitting to any test and. I don't indulge in drugs on any level. However, when I learned from the visitors who was also tested that day had been tested about 30 times because she has been filing complaints against the administration at Southport, and another elderly woman stated she was tested 11 times and they denied her visits twice because they said she tested positive for cocaine. Why? They had a problem with her husband. I realized I was a target and I do not trust the "Substance Detection/Ion Scan" will be accurate.

It was a confirmation for me the retaliation machine was at work. Their goal is to paint me as a druggie, paste my photo and flag my name in the computer so any institution I visit my name will be displayed flagged as a drug courier. That's a sick thing to do. They will eventually cease all of my visits, try to silence me and torture my nephew because I filed complaints against the Superintendent and the rest of the administration at Greenhaven Correctional facility. That blue wall is standing tall. It doesn't matter that they are fully aware of my MOS status, as well as my memoirs and complaints.

I firmly believe they will wait a couple of visits and be prepared to test me again in advance. They will give me the random story and already have a tainted cloth box just for me to place on the "Substance Detection/Ion Scan" machine. They will if they pretend it's a new fresh cloth outside the box. It will show with the results and they think there will be no way for me to fight it. Or while I am on the visit they will open my locker and plant something in it.

They have already started the retaliation on Delamar.

> 1. Greenhaven Correctional Facility has purposely withheld two bags of his legal work. He requested his legal work accompany him to Southport Correctional Facility when they transported him versus bags containing clothing. He needs his legal work to fight his case. Nevertheless they failed to deliver my nephew two remaining bags containing over $ 3000 worth of transcripts from the 3 consecutive trials he had in 2005.

> 2. Counselor Mischler refuses to assist him in the process. His cordial approach and concern to me on the telephone is the contradictory to the disrespects he inflicts upon Delamar when he inquires about locating his legal work. It's obvious he has no intention of doing the job he was hired to do. He needs to be investigated by an outside agency and all of the inmates he counsels needs to be interviewed. If he cannot set his personal prejudices aside, he needs to be removed.

> 3. Several weeks ago on a Friday, a Correction Officer was attempting to provoke Delamar by tightening the metal restraints around his body so tight. As he proceeded to tighten it he looked at my nephew and stated "What! You have a problem with that "Delamar remained silent. The next day, Saturday

Delamar prepared to go the yard. The officer on duty told him he couldn't go outside because his name was on the board for the draft Monday. I called Albany and his counselor Monday morning and learned he wasn't on the draft. He later learned and officer will place your name on the board so you could not go outside. An inmate is allowed one hour of recreation everyday. That is a direct violation of his rights.

4. When he first arrived at Southport they found a lighter in his cell. I believe it was planted. He was on keep lock for 30 days because of it.

5. The water in his cell is contaminated with a brown substance that runs from the faucet. I believe the administration are fully aware of the contaminated substance and simply do not care. They need the health department to investigate the water system.

I think my nephew has internal health issues as a result of that beating. The amount of body blows with the baton to his legs, back and spine.,could display detriment in the near future. At this point he remains silent. My fear is on the orders of Greenhaven administration; the Southport Correction Officers will beat him up and declare he assaulted staff. Why? His record now reflects those false charges of assaulting Correction Officers. What a cruel thing to do to a human being.

Delamar is presently in solitary confinement for something he did not do and that angers me. I worked for the Correction Department for 20 years. If an inmate in fact assaults any staff member they should definitely be penalized. However, I have seen too all too often inmates falsely accused by my colleagues and the system fails the inmates. Now I am witnessing the very system I worked for turn on me and my family member and that will be the driving force for me to speak out.

If Southport Correctional Facility employees want to prove retaliation against whistle blowing, abuse and prejudice is widespread throughout New York State correction facilities. I will be just the one to expose it. I refuse to be a target or disrespected because I have come forth with the truth.

Overall it's been difficult enough for Delamar be convicted of a crime he did not do. Our main focus has been obtaining legal representation to get his sentence overturned. That was his primary purpose for transferring to Greenhaven Correction facility. Not becoming a target for overzealous prejudice, ticking time bomb Correction Officers and an administration involved in concealing evidence to due to improper supervision. This is overall a travesty of justice.

In conclusion, I think it is disheartening that Acting Commissioner Anthony J Annucci would turn a blind eye to the evidence presented to him involving this case and condone the illegal acts performed by the administration due to cronyism. If that is in fact true Acting Commissioner Annucci needs to be investigated and removed.

Correction Officer Cefaloni and the administration covered-up the incident by falsifying documents. It's in black and white. That is why Delamar was never charged in the court of law because they flat out lied and there were no injuries to any officers. They also made sure it took almost 2 months for Delamar to see a physician. At this point everything is internal and I know they will never perform a MRI to show tissue damaged from all the blows he suffered at the hands of the Correction Officers at Greenhaven,

I am respectfully requesting to you requesting you investigate this matter thoroughly I have attached all of my documents from this case. Can you please have an outside agency that is not part of the cronyism circle look at his appeal? I am filing this document for further use if needed. I would like someone to view the documents from the incident with Delamar, the tape of them escorting him from his cell to the visit room on December 4, 2014. As well as Delamar's appeal and you will clearly see inconsistencies within the written and verbal hearing testimony, primarily Correction Officer Jamison's testimony validating and verifying Delamar's claim of not one but several Correction Officers beating him, statements, reports and diagrams. You will see Correction Officer Cefaloni falsified legal documents. Delamar did absolutely nothing before, during or after the assault. He never defended himself he just took the beating. He and his record are scarred. This will follow him the duration of his stay in the penal system, until I can get his sentence overturned. His blood is on everyone's hand in Greenhaven Correctional Facility.

This is a cruel and inhuman thing for those officers and administration and especially Acting Commissioner Anthony J Annucci can do. The Acting Commissioner needs to be replaced because this is not the first time this has happened in the New York State prison system since he became Commissioner.

My memoirs are about to be released I will be starting a book tour shortly and do not have a problem voicing my concerns with the media and social media. They will listen to me because of my status and be amazed at how they treat one of their own. We all took the same oath and the bad seeds need to be weeded out. I understand why visitors are frustrated with the process of the correctional facilities

In conclusion it's a sad day when the very agency I gave 20 years of my life to, turns their back on me when I seek assistance against this wrongdoing. You allowed business as usual to continue at Greenhaven Correctional Facility. I did not present theories or emotions. These are facts. When you allow a select few of Correction Officers seek to destroy and dismantle inmates for no reason whatsoever, other than hatred, racism and control. This is a recipe for disaster.

Greenhaven Correctional Facility will eventually have a murder at the hands of the Correction Officers. An outside agency needs to get in their quick and do a thorough investigation. Inspector General is coming up empty primarily because the inmates do not trust they will protect them. I just have one question. What will it take for someone to open up the transfer books and see how many uses of force Greenhaven Correctional Facility had in the last 3 years? How many inmates were transferred to Southport and Elmira for assaulting Correction Officers? How many inmates were indicted for assaulting Correction Officers? How many inmates refused medical attention? How many Correction Officers were hospitalized because of uses of force? These Correction Officers are lying, falsifying and covering up incidents and getting away with it. Just open up the files and you will see repeat Correction Officer Offenders. When does this matter? When an inmate or Correction Officer is murdered behind these actions?

Respectfully Submitted

Robin Kay Miller

Cc President Barack Obama,NYS Inspector General Cathy Leahy Scott

Civil Rights Attorney Norman Siegel,Federal Bureau Investigations

US Attorney's Office Civilian Crime Reports,Superintendent Sheahan Southport Correctional Facility,Office of Special Investigations – Investigator Ortiz,Acting Commissioner Anthony Annucci,Governor Andrew Cuomo,Senator Charles Schumer

*It didn't end there. They continued to utilize the drug ion scan on me for drugs at Southport Correctional Facility. Delamar was transferred out early to Great Meadow Correctional Facility, for good behavior. My first visit to that facility was degrading , intentional and disrespectful .

May 5, 2016

Dear Attorney General Loretta E Lynch,

My name is Robin K Miller. I am a retired New York City Correction Officer. This document is regarding Justice Department Delamar Brown (case ID# 2942366), the attempted murder on my nephew by Greenhaven Correction Officers, whistle blowing by Robin K Miller and retaliation via ion scan by both Southport Correctional Facility and presently Great Meadow Correctional Facility .

I have been a Correction Officer for 20 years and retired with an impeccable record. I am all too familiar with the procedures of a hit list. I used to sit with my colleagues, Captains, Deputy Wardens and on occasion Wardens and observe them in corruptive manners. I have also been subjected to an indirect retaliation when I filed an EEO suit against my superior officer prior to retiring and won.

It has become increasingly obvious there is a bull's eye on my back, as well as my nephew Delamar's back, as I stated in my previous document to you, Attorney General Lynch on June 16, 2015 (see attached) by the Greenhaven administration.

One of the methods being utilized is Ion scanning. I know there is no random selection. There is an entry in the master list in Albany with a big red flag next to my name. I was never drug scanned in Greenhaven Correctional Facility. However, immediately arriving at Southport I was subjected to numerous scans. Prompting me to submit a letter to you.

My nephew was recently transferred to Great Meadow Correctional Facility and my first visit was on Sunday May 1, 2016. I was subjected to an ION Scan after the female Correction Officer looked up my name in the leaflet on her desk. The male Correction Officer escorted me to the room whereas the scrutiny of my flesh and attire would be examined. The ION scanning resorted to a degraded level.

This time I was subjected to inside hands, outside hands, up and down pant leg, top of footwear, pant pockets and the last straw was when the Correction Officer conducting the scan told me to hold my arms up, and turn around. I was appalled, but I complied. I was waiting for him to tell me to bend down, squat and cough. I have never been so humiliated in my life. I dedicated my entire life to be a Correction Officer manning some of the most dangerous criminals, some of which are in the New York State facilities, and to be subjected to the continuous lack of respect, by the prison system employees (city and state) is disheartening.

I suspect Captain Cary and Superintendent Griffin from Greenhaven Correctional Facility are behind this disrespect. I have visited my nephew throughout the years and never been subjected to this scanning process. Both of these superior officers are well known, have ties to Albany, family members in high places and as powerful as New York Assembly Speaker Sheldon Silver once was, until the bricks begun to unfold.

I have a strong suspicion my nephew, family members and I will be a consistent target while in Great Meadow Correctional Facility, with a false drug scanning read to deter us from visiting him. The reason I suspect these actions is because he was housed in Great Meadow several years ago and his urine was compromised by the Correction Officers looking to make some side cash. He informed me via telephone prior to being transferred to solitary confinement. I immediately wrote the State Inspector General because of the corruptive behavior by the correction officers. In return, retaliation ensued and all of his clothing was destroyed (via doused with baby oil) by the correction officers at Great Meadow and my nephew stopped speaking to me and never informed me of any corruption until he was almost killed by the Correction Officers in Greenhaven Correctional Facility.

There is a no snitch policy in the prison system. Inmates are not allowed to snitch on correction officers or punishment is involved. I know all too well how Correction Officers plant knives, weapons, drugs, switch urine, and get other inmates to beat or shank you. I know the shenanigans. My nephew is against me submitting this document. He feels it is going to get worse. My sentiments are: It has already gotten worse. I was disgraced in the ION scanning process and all of his clothing is missing from his property. As I stated in the document written to you, on June 16, 2015, upon his arrival at Southport Correctional Facility, his property (clothing) was not transferred. He had no way of knowing because he was in wrongfully placed in solitary confinement. I shipped a food package that he will probably not receive for 2-3 weeks, along with his mail.

In conclusion I am respectfully requesting an investigation ensue and want to know why my name has a red flag in the master system. The fact that my name, and any of my family members names, have an asterisk next to it, confirms, this is retaliation and the justice department needs to get involved.

I am filing a lawsuit for discrimination, prejudice and retaliation for whistle blowing against New York State employees.

As I stated in my previous reports I am penning my memoirs and it is about my tenure as a New York City Correction Officer and now post retirement. I will not allow anyone to discredit my character. I do not drink, or indulge in any form of drugs or illegal activities. My family has become prey in the prison system.

My memoirs will be released in a couple of weeks. I am about to resume my media tour with New York Post, Nightline World News, CNN 360 Anderson Cooper & CNN Poppy Harlow, to name a few. I am in talks about a movie and TV series. Corruption in the prison system is real and I have been subjected to it and refuse to allow the prison system to violate and disrespect me or my family. If you Google my name you will see every written and visual interview.

Can you please instruct the justice department to look into this matter? It appears abuse of power underway in Albany's master computer, and a retired New York City Correction Officer is the target for reporting corruption.

Respectfully Submitted

Robin K Miller

CC:

President Barack Obama

US Department of Justice Preet Bharara

Civil Rights Attorney Norman Siegel

Superintendent Christopher Miller Great Meadow Correctional Facility

CNN Anderson Cooper, Exoneration Initiative

My suggestion is: document every occurrence. Once you start filing complaints, you must continue. Yes, you can make calls to Albany, but you have no idea who they are connected to. Start a paper trail because it may save your loved ones life.

CHAPTER 13

MENTAL HEALTH

You would be surprised to learn that over 50% of the people thrown into Solitary Confinement either develop or already suffer from mental illness. This is a touchy subject, so touchy I think people should take mental illness in prison seriously and not toy with it. When I say toy, I am referring to, the people who enter the prison system and use mental health as part of their defense, pleading temporary insanity, attempting to avoid prosecution.

In my opinion, given the right or wrong situation, we are all prone to display crazy behavior. I do not believe inmates who are mentally disturbed should reside on Rikers Island. They should be in a facility that strictly caters to mentally disturbed prisoners. Nevertheless in the event they have to reside in prison, a Correction Officer who lacks the knowledge of handling that type of prisoner, should not be guarding that particular prisoner, under any circumstances. Many clinically mentally disturbed individuals are not in control of their behavior and can become verbally and physically abusive. If a Correction Officer thinks gang style beatings, ignoring or putting a mentally disturbed inmate into solitary confinement is key to controlling them, they are sadly mistaken.

According to many city and state facilities inmate on correction officer assaults are at an all time high. If an inmate assaults a Correction Officer for any reason unexpectedly, it is obvious there are some mental health issues. That is not normal behavior unless they are being provoked or correction officers are stating these actions are occurring to cover their tracks because they used excessive force on an inmate .

I worked with many emotionally challenged inmates throughout my career as a correction officer. When I worked in the Brooklyn Court Division, the only way to communicate with them as they awaited their court appearance, was to please their pleasures and try to keep them as calm as possible. When I say please their pleasures, I am referring to getting them a cigarette and institutional food (cheese/meat sandwich). The majority of the time if they had those two items, they were calm. "C O give me a cigarette "would echo throughout the holding pens in the Brooklyn Court Facility I worked in. If you did not get them a cigarette, they would threaten to cut their wrist, and look for and find something to cut themselves.

Right before I retired, they banned cigarettes and that made my job a little harder. To be quite honest, I was scared to death because you can see for the most part they were dangerous and could snap at any time. I would try to talk to them and figure out how to keep them calm. You simply do not know.

Analyzing the current prison system and thinking about my 20-year stint as a correction officer, I know there has to be a connection between correction officers using excessive force on an inmates via beating inmates in the head with flashlights, batons, fist and feet and mental illness. Mental Health and Solitary Confinement goes hand in hand. If you place any person in isolation from human contact for twenty three to twenty four hours a day, what do you expect will happen? Eventually their mind will start playing tricks on them, and that is when they begin conversing with themselves. I mean, literally having long conversations; the kind of conversations when you ask and answer yourself.

You have inmates in all these segregation statuses calling it protective custody, administration segregation and punitive segregation. You are confining them to coffin like residences. They are barely eating, they have no reading material and shower maybe once a week. All of that together is toxic for the mind. Eventually the hallucinating begins; once your mind snaps; there will most likely be no turning back.

The police are arresting people with mental illness and they are stuck in the jails. Some of the Correction Officers are so insensitive to the fact that these prisoners are sick mentally. They treat them like shit and do not keep an eye on them.

Prime example is the Rikers Island mentally disturbed inmate who was homeless died in his cell. It is my opinion; if the Correction Officer conducted their mandatory security checks. The inmate might be alive today. The sad part is some of the correction officers are extremely insensitive.

Check this conversation out. I went back and forth with this correction officer. I will leave out their names of the active duty correction officers. This is an old posting that was immediately taken down. The purpose; these correction officers need sensitivity training.

Robin K Miller - According to the city officials, Murdough was locked alone into his 6-by-10 cinderblock cell at about 10:30 p.m. on Feb. 14, a week after his arrest. Because he was in the mental-observation unit, he was SUPPOSED TO BE CHECKED EVERY 15 MINUTES AS PART OF SUICIDE WATCH, they said. But MURDOUGH was NOT DISCOVERED until FOUR HOURS LATER, at about 2:30 a.m. on Feb. 15. He was slumped over in his bed and already dead. I SAY YES! As a retired officer, I would sue the pants off NYCDOC. I am quite sure if it was any member of DOC they know the program and would know they didn't do security checks. Right is right, wrong is wrong

Officer #1 - Let's move on! Old news!!!!

Robin K. Miller If this was your son would you want to move on. Are your loved ones old news if they die in the care of other people? How insensitive.

Officer #2 There's nothing insensitive about it his family allow him to

145

live in the streets, he try to find warmth in an housing project, he was arrested for sleeping trespassing in a public housing staircase, he was brought in front of a judge who remanded him just for trying to stay warm in a public housing staircase, comes to corrections Corizon says he's bipolar and gives him meds and he dies in a hot cell. The city is truly not in full fault here.

Officer #2 Some people are cold as ice

Robin K. Miller I see the only was XXXXX the story would change is if it was your family member. Then again maybe you are so cold inside it would still not matter. He was mentally ill. What part do you not understand? MENTALLY ILL. Do you have mentally ill people in your family? The officers didn't do their 15 minute security checks. That is why 4 hours later he was found. Isn't the feeding at 5am? That is why they discovered them at 4:30 am. They probably were sleeping on the midnight tour. I would bet you they were brought up on charges. Would he be alive or not? Who knows? If it was my family member, I don't care if they were a mentally ill person, crack head, dope fiend. I would want answers. Don't tell me you do not care because he is a black man. I hope that's not your issue.

Officer #2 When it comes to *Officer #3* who doesn't think he's black. It could be the issue (just saying)

Officer #3 Even I the officer was touring was she able to save his life? Does she carry a thermometer to check the cells temperature? Is there a temperature setting/indicator stating the temperature of the cell? First and foremost I have no family members living in the streets sorry bit my family will not stand for that and this is why none of them are in the streets. IF he was bipolar then help him do not allow him to roam the streets while your living in another state nice and warm. I'm not insensitive I'm expressing my view of the accounts to why they try to blame a lonely correction officer who does not have the tools to combat this type of incident. Touring or no touring would changed this outcome that's why it was called an accident!

Officer #4 @Robin you're right mentally ILL therefore should've been in a mental institution not rikers!!! His family don't care he's dead!! I wonder how many time they visited him at rikers!! Most likely "NONE" but now they care because they're about to hit the ghetto lottery!!!

Officer #2 Exactly

Officer #4 Correction officer!!! Not a doctor, psych, electrician!!! A tour wasn't going to save his life!!! Why not blame the government for not giving a veteran his fair treatment!!! If his mental condition was so severe why wasn't he a 1on1 inmate!!! The island has become a money making machine thanks to the liberals of the state!!!! Ghetto lottery ticket for most!!! Smh

Guy #1 @ *Officer #1* you sound like a fool

This is the end of this blog. It was taken down but I was able to copy it before it was deleted. Numerous Correction Officers are so insensitive and judgmental it makes me sick to my stomach.

They are not grasping what mental illness is. These Correction Officers were ready to curse me out for speaking out. To me it was more about race than anything was. When you see terminology like **ghetto** lottery, it is obvious.

A person can come to jail under unfortunate circumstance and poof their lives are ruined. The longer they stay in jail the more they lose on the outside and that has to affect them mentally. Topple that with dealing with the day-to-day-overzealous egotistical bully correction officer who like to treat inmates like crap; can make a sound-minded person crack, and other inmates who are ruined as well.

What people fail to realize is that New York State Prisons offer little to no programs and have nothing for the majority of these inmates to do. That is why violence has a place in the jail. The inmate are not pre-occupied with anything constructive, sitting in a cell all day with nothing to do, that weighs heavily on them mentally. The prison system is creating mental health patients and tossing them back onto the streets.

My solution to handling the mental health inmates is to hire people with a degree in mental health. These people should have at least 5 years experience working with mental health patients and still have the passion for it. Train them as a correction officer and pay them extra. Once they graduate, their only assignment will be working in a building that is designated for mental health patients only. They will only deal with mental health patients their entire careers. What a sad state of affairs all of this is.

CHAPTER 14

TODAY'S RIKERS

Today's Rikers culture continues: Messy, messy, and hot messy. It was messy in the 80's and its funky now. It is unbelievable how much turmoil and corruption still exist and has escalated to a disgusting embarrassing level. To the point, it becomes increasingly uncomfortable for any decent active duty or retired correction officer, who plays by all the rules, to acknowledge they are actually a member of the force. It has to make you cringe to display your shield and identification card proudly.

I have not been on Rikers in years and judging from all the media coverage, articles in the newspapers and convictions of correction, ranking officers and ex-commissioners it is not headed for disaster, it is a disaster.

New York City Department of Correction - Rikers Island overall is a train wreck. CNN's Anderson Cooper captioned "Who's watching the Joint" on my July 2nd interview with him, about state correction. My answer to that: no one is watching the joint in state or city corrections. It reeks of more of the same pathetic chaotic corruption ignored by the higher ups.

So here, we are thirty years later, since I became a correction officer and the behavior of the correction employees is not just more of the same; its worse, far worse, than anyone could imagine.

They are still openly hiring criminals. Who in the world is doing the hiring? For starters, who vetted and appointed ex-Commissioner Bernard Kerik, to be in charge of the correction department in the previous decade? No commissioner or ex-commissioner has ever gone to jail.

Who was in charge of hiring gang members to become correction officers; then again, that is nothing new. If they are not gang member entering the job, they form or join their own gang once employed? Prime example is the secret sadistic society called "The Program", where the guards ordered prisoners to extort and beat other prisoners.

For many years, corruption has been plaguing the prisons like a cancer with alleged correction officer rapes and the guards convicted of drug, alcohol & weapon smuggling and excessive inmate beatings or negligence resulting in inmate deaths.

I became a correction officer in the early eighties. Each decade the behavior has become more twisted, ratchet and sadistic. The term they do not believe shit stinks even when smeared in their face applies more so today; because the Correction Officers have become more, bolder and invincible throughout the years. Look at the sign when you enter Rikers Island "HOME OF NEW YORK'S BOLDEST", in all caps. Wow !

They are blaming the new correction officers, but if you look at many of the convictions, the culprits are tenured officers hired in the eighties and nineties. Not for nothing, they made the environment hazardous for the current correction officers to properly do their jobs.

The past decades of abuse of power, excessive force, murders and rapes inflicted on inmates has created an atmosphere whereas; I had better get them before they get me, is the mindset of today's prisoner.

We will not know if the culture from the decades prior to 2010 has continued, unless the media reports it. It appears the Correction Officers hired prior to 2010 seem to be the ones committing all the in-house jail crimes.

As I stated in my earlier chapters, I place some of the blame on the administration's failure to take charge and supervise. No, matter how you slice it. Correction Officers watch the prisoners and the ranking officers are supposed to watch the correction officers and inmates. That is why they get the big bucks. Utilizing your communication skills is key, to a safer, tour of duty; it is as simple as that.

Countless correction officers shun their colleagues for communicating with prisoners respectively. They are labeled inmate lover and stagnates the process of reforming. Some ranking officers believe it is beneath them to converse with anyone below their rank. Therefore they linger clueless and in the dark.

My use of utilizing my communication skills in a male prison was the solution to my safety. When you consistently speak to a prisoner in a respectful manner, they are more likely than not respect and protect you. (Keep in mind we are outnumbered), they will make sure your tour of duty runs smoothly.

If the ranking officers would consistently communicate with the Correction Officers and make frequent visits to housing areas and get into the psyche of these correction officers. They might be able to pinpoint who has corrupt tendencies. I hope these ranking officers are not sitting in their offices playing games cell phones; bitching about who has submitted an infraction on an inmate and now they have to do paperwork; like many used to do.

Our union President Norman Seabrook stated in an interview whereas an inmate was beat down and filed suit:" These correction Officers are doing everything asked of them."

Therefore, my question is to our union President. Who is asking them to shed darkness and shame on the department? Some of these correction officers are doing exactly what they were verbally and physically, influenced and encouraged to do. While others are forced to participate and if they do not, retaliation will rear its ugly head.

On the other hand, you have a small minority winging it and going solo on their corruption schemes. Sadly enough, there is a minority that is doing the right thing and suffering public shame because of theses bad apples.

Do not get me wrong you have some good correction officers that are a great influence. I met many during my journey. I am not talking about them. I am talking about the ones who are bringing disgrace to the correction department.

I was on the inside, I was that rookie officer once and I know how things go. I saw it up close and personal. I know all about this taking you under the wingy thingy goes. Its human nature for people to want to fit in and the only difference with me was; I was a leader not a follower and I refused to participate; if it meant taking food off my table and placing handcuffs on my wrist..

I did not care about fitting in, cliques or multiple friends. I didn't frequent the correction officer functions, parties or bars gatherings.

Believe me when I say; the culture from my era and probably before my era, has definitely extended itself to the present. Nowadays it is a deep-seated culture of drug peddling, sexual abuse, murder and violence.

These new recruits are reminiscent of when you are rearing a child and molding them. They watch you like a hawk and mimic your every move. You do not realize it until you observe them without their knowledge. It is like invasion of the body snatchers. The rookie officer takes on the outward appearance and actions of the senior officer like a contagious virus.

It is not just the correction officers; some of these Captains are personally involved in some of these excessive forces on inmate situations. One question; How do you not, participate in an inmate beat down when your superior officer orders it?

As far as the allege correction officer rapes and the ones convicted of drugs, alcohol, weapon smuggling and excessive inmate beatings or negligence resulting in inmate deaths. I cannot begin to process the **mindset** of how such an act begins.

You expect an inmate to partake in criminal acts; not a law enforcement official that has taken an oath to uphold the law. Stupidity, greed and character issues are to blame for these brainless corrupt acts. As far as I am concerned, that has nothing to do with the job. It is a core moral issue.

So on that note let us look at this mess throughout the years. Please keep in mind; this is reported corruption. There is still corruption unreported.

Beating Reports Probed At Rikers Island Jail

August 17, 1990 City officials are investigating allegations that guards at Rikers Island jail lined up and clubbed inmates in retaliation for a three-hour melee. Robert Kasanof, chairman of the Board of Correction, said he had compiled "significant evidence" that guards beat inmates at random several hours after Tuesday night's uprising. The inmates apparently were angry because guards had blockaded the jail for two days. The guards were protesting prison violence and what they called overly lenient treatment of inmates.

Rikers Guard Is Accused Of Arranging to Be Shot

July 23, 1993 At first, Correction Officer Tommy Jones sounded like a hero. Officer Jones, a guard at a Rikers Island jail, said that he had been shot in the thigh while single-handedly breaking up a melee among 48 inmates on Jan. 2. But yesterday he was arrested and charged with having arranged for two inmates to shoot him to cover up his role in a tangled gun-smuggling plot. Mr. Jones, 23, a correction officer since 1990, became worried in January that he would be implicated when the shootings took place and asked the inmates to shoot him, too, when they wounded themselves, New York City's Investigation Commissioner Ms. Shepard said. Another correction officer, Roger A. Morice, smuggled a .22-caliber derringer into the George R. Vierno Correctional Center on Rikers Island late last year for two inmates awaiting trials on murder charges. Officer Morice was promised $3,000 to $5,000 for bringing in the weapon, Ms. Shepard said.

Rikers Officers Are Arrested In a Drug Sting

March 21, 1995 Four correction officers and two cooks on Rikers Island were arrested yesterday and charged with smuggling cocaine to inmates at city jails in exchange for bribes. The correction officers charged with smuggling narcotics were Joseph Gaines, 30, of the Bronx; Sheldon Boyd, 29, of Queens; Veronica Clarke, 30, of Brooklyn, and Jonathan Sirera, 30, of the Bronx

Yesterday's arrests bring to 26 the number of Rikers employees charged since 1990 with smuggling narcotics to prisoners, highlighting the flow of drugs to Rikers Island and the lure of money for jail employees willing to act as drug couriers. As part of the same investigation, two other Rikers officers were arrested yesterday on drug-dealing charges unrelated to the jails.

Papers Say Guards Beat Inmates At Rikers Island

August 17, 1998 Inmates at the Rikers Island jail complex for years have been subjected to impromptu beatings and planned assaults by guards, according to court papers. In the past decade, Rikers inmates have been brutally beaten, suffering broken bones, ruptured eardrums or severe head injuries, The New York Times reported Sunday. Details of the beatings emerged from court papers, mainly as a result of a recent court settlement that spelled out reforms. New York City Department of Correction officials said they agreed to settle a class-action suit by 15 inmates to ward off greater restrictions on the jail.

EX-JAIL GUARD PLEADS GUILTY IN TEEN PORN CASE

January 10, 2005 A former Rikers Island corrections officer is headed up the river himself for trying to seduce teenage boys over the Internet, prosecutors said. Jeffrey Skya, 47, faces up to six months in jail after pleading guilty Friday to sending pornographic images over the Internet to a 15-year-old boy in Nassau County. The Bethpage dad was nabbed in August 2003 during an Internet sex sting. Skya, who lives with his mom and two teenage sons, had numerous sex chats with an investigator posing as a 14-year-old that summer, prosecutors said. When the jail guard showed up at a park to meet his underaged "date," cops collared him on the spot. Assistant Nassau District Attorney Stephen Treglia said Skya arrived at the rendezvous with lubricant and a condom. Skya was immediately charged with three counts of attempted dissemination of indecent material to minors. District attorney's office investigators then executed a search warrant of Skya's America Online E-mail account and discovered Skya had sent a photo of a penis to a 15-year-old boy. The lewd picture led the district attorney to charge Skya - whose screen name was "XXRated" - with disseminating indecent material to minors. Treglia said that he hopes Skya's conviction "sends a message that if you're out there doing this sort of messaging with minors, we'll do everything we can to catch you. Skya's Seventh St. neighbors seemed relieved by the guilty plea. "As long as he's found guilty, he has to register as a sex offender. That's a good thing," said a neighbor with children. "He is who he is. At least now it's out there, and he can't hide behind anything.

DOI ARREST CORRECTION CAPTAIN FOR SEXUALLY ABUSING INMATES.

January 2006 Captain Dominick Labruzzi allegedly took the eight inmates between the ages of 16 and 19 on 10 separate occasions to a secluded, locked area within [the Adolescent Reception and Detention Center] and allegedly inappropriately touched the inmates' genitals through their clothing, forced them to disrobe, asked them to stand or squat before him, and fondled some inmates' genitals or buttocks." Captain Dominick Labruzzi accepted his punishment plea bargained and was sentenced to a three-year-probation sentence in 2010.

***This guy is a sicko. No jail time whatsoever.

GUARD AT RIKERS TO GET 2 YRS. IN DRUG AND BRIBE RAP

May 22, 2006 A Rikers Island correction officer is expected to be sentenced today to two years behind bars for taking a bribe and attempting to sell cocaine to an inmate. Gary Heyward, 38, confessed to accepting a $500 payment from an inmate on Jan. 21 to smuggle a cell phone into the jail and to delivering the phone to the prisoner the next day. Three days later, Heyward accepted $1,000 from the same inmate in exchange for a bag containing a white, powdery substance that Heyward believed to be more than an ounce of cocaine. Heyward was one of five Department of Correction employees and one Health and Hospitals Corp. employees arrested for allegedly smuggling drugs and contraband into city jail facilities. Correction Officer Glenda Glenn was first to face criminal charges for cigarette smuggling since the new rules were enacted in March 2003. She said a single cigarette could fetch $10 to $20.

*** She is just stupid, she needs her ass whipped.

6-Year Sentence for Guard in Rikers Island "The Program" Beatings

April 2008 Prosecutors had charged the guard, Lloyd Nicholson, 38, of Mount Vernon, N.Y., with gang assault and said he had ordered six inmates to beat two others in 2007 as part of a rogue disciplinary system that he and other guards called "The Program." One of the beaten inmates, Michael Twiggs, suffered a punctured lung. An 18-year-old inmate at the Davoren Center, Christopher Robinson, was beaten to death by other inmates, the authorities have said. Mr. Nicholson both watched and participated and allowed inmates to extort commissary and telephone privileges from their peers. . On August. 6, 2010 sentenced to 6 years in jail and 5 years probation.

Rikers Guards Accused of Passing Contraband to Inmate

July 2008 Rookie Correction Officers Auguste Durand 31 and Michael Santiago 24 delivered marijuana, rolling papers, cigarettes and an occasional swig of booze to cop killing inmate Lee Woods. Inmate Lee Woods was also found in possession of a handcuff key and sim card. They were both fired.

Correction officer busted in prison peddle of drugs and tobacco

November 2010 Correction Officer Clarence Carrier, 45, was nabbed inside the Anna M. Kross Center with 30 Suboxone pills and eight pouches of tobacco and had intended to sell the tobacco to jailbirds for $20 a pouch and was going to deliver the Suboxone pills to an inmate for an undisclosed amount of cash. Suboxone is used to treat painkiller addiction.

Rikers Correction Officer Sentenced For Taking Inmate's $100K Cocaine Bribe

April 2011, Corrections officer Robert Whitfield has been found guilty of drug possession, conspiracy, bribery and official misconduct and helping an inmate escape for $100.000 worth of cocaine. Correction Officer Whitfield had bragged that he could alter the inmate's records by accessing a New York City Department of Correction computer

***This goes on a lot in the court facilities.

Rikers Captain, Guards Fired For Hogtying And Beating Inmate

April 3, 2012. The Department of Correction has fired a captain and five correction officers for hogtying and beating a handcuffed, mentally ill inmate in 2012.. The inmate, Robert Hinton, emerged from the beating with a broken nose and vertebrae, a bleeding mouth, and eyes swollen shut. An investigation revealed that the captain, Budnarine Behari, and Officers Geronimo Almanzar, Vincent Siederman, Paul Bunton, Ramon Cabrera, and Raul Marquez, entered Hinton's cellblock on April 3rd, 2012, cuffed him, beat him and choked him, allegedly because he protested being denied a baloney sandwich. Jail surveillance cameras showed the corrections officers carrying a hogtied and handcuffed Hinton into his solitary confinement cell. The beating, which lasted about 10 minutes, was not caught on video. This guy was awarded 6 figures and died the day before they cut the check.

Guard convicted in NYC inmate's 2012 death

August 2012 A New York jury Wednesday convicted Terrence Pendergrass, 50, on a civil rights charge for ignoring dying inmate Jason Echevarria. Prosecutors say was the captain on duty when Jason Echevarria swallowed a so-called prison soap ball made of corrosive ammonium chloride in 2012 and died in agony because Pendergrass failed to act by getting him medical attention. Left unattended for hours in spite of his screams, Echevarria was discovered dead the following day

UPDATE- June 18, 2015 Today, former Rikers Island captain Terrence Pendergrass was sentenced to five years in prison for denying medical attention to an inmate who died after swallowing a toxic detergent packet. When coworkers expressed concern about the inmate, Pendergrass reportedly replied, "Don't bother me unless someone is dead."

Rikers Guard Sodomized Inmate with Flashlight, Says Complaint

November 24, 2012, Correction Officer Gregory Lewis pulled inmate Anthony Wallace, 26, out of a medication line for a search. The process began standard enough: strip down, bend over, spread cheeks. The search took a heinous turn: correction officer Gregory Lewis allegedly removed a flashlight from his belt and "forcefully shoved the flashlight" into Wallace's anus.

***This is disgusting Correction Officer Gregory Lewis is a pervert. Who cleared him for duty? FIRE THEM.

FBI Arrests Two New York Correction Officers in Alleged Beating Death of Inmate

December 2012

FBI agents on Wednesday morning arrested two New York correction officers in the beating death of a Rikers Island inmate, according to the agency. The medical examiner's office last year concluded that 52-year-old inmate Ronald Spear, a pretrial detainee, died in December 2012 from blunt force trauma to the head, Then last year, New York City paid $2.75 million to settle a lawsuit about the death of Spear, who had kidney problems and walked with a cane. Spear was being treated for dialysis while at Rikers. Sometimes he was treated at the prison clinic or was taken to outside medical facilities for care. Coll "willfully kicked Ronald Spear multiple times in the head while he was restrained, which resulted in injury to Spear," according to the complaint. At the time, Spear was lying facedown on the prison floor. The document says that Coll told Spear, "Remember that I'm the one who did this to you." Then he dropped Spear on his head on the hard prison floor. The complaint alleges that Coll and Taylor "agreed to make false statements to multiple investigators about the assault of Ronald Spear...in order to cover up the fact that Coll had unlawfully assaulted Spear." Coll joined the New York City Department of Correction in 2002 and Taylor in 2012.

Rikers Island guard convicted of smuggling in drugs to sell to inmates

June 2013 Correction Officers Austin Romain and Khalif Phillip both 31 were arrested for smuggling drugs and scalpels into a maximum security wing. November 14, 2014 Khalif Phillip was sentenced to 3 years.

***Making $100,000 a year and that wasn't enough. Really dudes a scalpel. One of your fellow officers could have been killed.

Rikers Island Correction Officers Accused Of Trafficking Drugs Into Prison

June 2014 Correction Officers Steven Dominguez and Divine Rahming, each had book bags and smuggled cocaine and oxycodone into Rikers Island with the help of an inmate's girlfriend They were also charged with conspiracy, bribery and drug possession. . Another former Rikers guard, Deleon Gifth, who resigned earlier this year, was arrested Monday on charges that he was paid $500 to deliver what he thought was oxycodone to an inmate back in February. CO Dominguez and Mr. Rahming were also offering to help provide protection for the transportation of cocaine outside the jail.

Female Inmates Raped and Abused by Rikers Island Guards, Lawsuit Claims

May 20, 2015 Seven correction officers at Rikers Island raped and sexually abused female inmates over a two-year period, according to a federal lawsuit filed Tuesday by the Legal Aid Society. Two of the female inmates were in pre-trial custody, and they allege they were "repeatedly raped and sexually abused" by an officer who warned they would be punished if they resisted or reported him, the lawsuit said.

Legal Aid Society attorney William Gibney said there is credible evidence to back up the inmates' claims, including clothing from one woman that contained DNA material from an officer proving a sex act took place. In another case, he said, an inmate became pregnant.. In the lawsuit filed in federal court in Manhattan, the women alleged numerous sex attacks took place inside the Rose M. Singer Center on Rikers, which houses female inmates. The incidents allegedly took place in 2013 and 2014, and some were reported immediately after they happened. In one case, a female inmate alleges she became pregnant from one of the alleged rapes. In another case, an inmate alleges an officer molested her in front of other officers and was terminated only after he was arrested for smuggling marijuana into the facility. The rapes allegedly took place in an inmate's cell or the "officers' station," the complaint alleges. . One woman who complained was assigned to "punitive segregation" and some inmates were allegedly paid to beat up any woman who complained of a sexual assault.

*CASE IS PENDING. THESE ARE ALLEDGED ACTS.

Correction Officer Accused of Smuggling Contraband Into Manhattan Detention Complex

June 18, 2015 A New York City correction officer, an inmate and two relatives have been accused of smuggling contraband into the Manhattan Detention Complex, law enforcement officials said on Thursday. The correction officer, Patricia Howard, 44, was arrested last month after prosecutors said she was found carrying nine grams of cocaine, three ounces of marijuana, four cellphones, tobacco, rolling papers, pliers and a flashlight in a red shopping bag. She intended to smuggle the items to an inmate at the detention complex in Lower Manhattan, where she worked,.The investigation, which included wiretaps and the use of an undercover investigator, found that Ms. Howard, a correction officer for nearly 20 years, would bring contraband into the jail.

New York City Corrections Officer with gang ties busted for selling heroin in Queens, cops say

Wednesday, July 8, 2015

Earlier today, a total of 12 members and associates of the Bloods street gang located in Queens, New York, including Covel Duncan, a New York City Corrections Officer at Riker's Island, were arrested on narcotics trafficking charges. Covel Duncan, 30, who worked at Rikers Island, was arrested with along with Shavona Trappier. Agents seized 500 glassines of heroin and $7,000 in cash in their home, officials said. A source said Duncan was supplied with heroin by Lambus and Trappier, and then she allegedly peddled the junk in the jail. Duncan faces a maximum term of imprisonment of 20 years and no minimum term of imprisonment.

Rikers Guards Allegedly Orchestrated And Covered Up Assault On Inmate

Sep 18, 2015 Two Rikers correction officers are facing up to seven years in prison for allegedly convincing four inmates to assault a fellow prisoner last January, and then filing false paperwork in an attempt to cover it up. The NY Times reports that Officers Nakia Gales, 39, and Herman Jiminian, 41, allegedly recruited four inmates at the Vernon C. Bain Center, a jail barge at Rikers called "the Boat," to beat up inmate Gilbert Bacallao after he "talked trash" to a third officer. According to court documents, Gales has "ties" to the Bloods gang, as do two of the four inmates she recruited. Gales, who was arraigned yesterday, pled not guilty to assault, falsifying records, and official misconduct. The News reports that she allegedly "lured" Bacallo into an empty vestibule in the Boat, claiming that there was a package waiting for him there. Bacallo was locked inside the vestibule, where four inmates were waiting to attack him. Gales allegedly watched the whole incident from her perch inside an operations-and-control room.

The two officers then filed a false "use of force" report. According to Capital, it stated that Bacallo had attacked Gales in the vestibule, and that Jiminian had intervened to help her.

Rikers Island Guard Nicole Bartley Busted For Rape, Smuggling Drugs

02.08.16 A New York City prison guard might soon find herself on the other side of the bars.

Nicole Bartley, a corrections officer at New York's Rikers Island facility, was charged on Sunday with raping a prisoner and conspiring to bring him marijuana. Bartley, who says she was in love with the inmate, was found out when a drug-sniffing dog caught a whiff of marijuana on her outside the prison.

Bartley has confessed to having sex with the Rikers inmate, who cannot legally consent while imprisoned.

"I was in love with him. He used me and played me for a fool. I had sex with him on one occasion in the jail a few days before Jan. 30," Bartley told investigators in a criminal complaint published by The New York Times. "I used a condom. It was in the closet in the morning when everyone else was locked in. It only lasted five minutes." But the charges against Bartley reveal a larger culture of contraband and sexual abuse at Rikers Island.

"I was fooled by Dasmond Loveless," Bartley testified, naming the inmate she assaulted. "I, Nicole, being a fool had my guard down to this man I thought [I] was falling in love with."

Despite Bartley's claims that their sexual relations were "mutual," Penal Law states that inmates like Loveless cannot legally consent to sex. As a corrections officer, Bartley faces third-degree rape charges for the alleged abuse of power.

She faces charges of third degree rape, sexual misconduct, official misconduct, promoting prison contraband, and fourth degree criminal possession of marijuana.

17 arrested - including correction officers in contraband smuggling takedown at Rikers Island

Thursday, May 19, 2016 Seventeen people - including Rikers Island inmates and correction officers -- were arrested Thursday as part of a takedown of a contraband smuggling operation at Rikers Island.

Those arrested included two New York City Department of Correction officers, a DOC-employed cook and six inmates. Prosecutors said they conspired to bring scalpels, narcotics and other contraband into the jail in exchange for thousands of dollars in bribes.

"Aside from tarnishing his badge by taking bribes from inmates, Correction Officer Kevin McKoy allegedly smuggled in scalpels," Bronx District Attorney Darcel Clark said in a news release. "Even after his fellow Correction Officer, Ray Calderon, was slashed on his face requiring 20 stitches and photos of his grisly wound were publicized, McKoy allegedly continued to bring in these weapons."

The DA said the main conspiracy involved McKoy, 31, who also went by nicknames of "The Plug," "Ticks-and-Fleas" and other names, and worked in the Quad "12 Upper" housing area at Rikers. Inmates would allegedly call friends and family members, telling them to give contraband and cash to McKoy. He'd then bring in scalpels wrapped in duct tape to avoid metal detectors, synthetic marijuana (K2) and suboxone (opioid) strips to inmates, the prosecutor said. In all, he made at least $10,000 on the deals.

Need I say more? The saga continues. I am flabbergasted and saddened. As you can see, the culture has definitely continued. Many of these correction officers have gotten bolder and dumber. The hiring process is rigged. Who is in charge of the physiological test? They are hiring felons, gang bangers, mentally disturbed and drug dealers. So where do we go from here. You need to form a justice department covert operation consisting of inmates and correction officers and flood the system, with them. No city employee should be privy to the identity of these plants. These rogue correction officers are placing everyone's life in danger; inmates and officers alike. I stress, these are cases that are openly reported .There has to be so much more.

CHAPTER 15

NEW YORK STATE CORRECTIONS

I think its high time the entire world focus on New York State Correctional facilities. Enough is enough. There is so much racial torture and gang-style plantation beatings transpiring every single day at the hands of the Correction Officers and no one seems to care.

Unfortunately as soon as I retired my nephew was incarcerated in a New York State prison. I've visited my nephew at Attica , Great Meadows and Greenhaven Correctional Facilities.

Out of courtesy and respect, I've always identified myself upon entering any facility as a retired correction officer.

Contrary to what people might think or say, because I am writing this book; I don't hate correction officers, and respect what they do. It's a hard job and there are some great officers out there; past and present.

Prior to this Greenhaven incident, hearsay about state prison conditions and corruption would have been my squabble.

Greenhaven Correctional puts the "C" in corruption. After my nephews ordeal, I decided to investigate and research Greenhaven Correctional facility.

The facility made headlines in the summer of 2014 regarding a correction officer's drug bust. They changed Superintendent's and instead of the new superintendent addressing the horrible conditions at this facility. It's alleged the correction officers openly boast he gave the green light to whip inmates asses.

I ruffled their feathers with my complaints. They were also shook when Civil Right Attorney Norman Siegel came to visit my nephew; (God Bless him)

Unfortunately my mother was murdered on April 24, 1973 , when I was 11 years old, and the people involved were never brought to justice. In 1986, unfortunately, my sister, a former NYC Correction Officer was introduced to the (take it one time and your hooked drug) crack-cocaine , by none other than New York's Boldest, her senior colleagues.

They climbed the ranks to become superior officers. She died in 2005, still battling her drug abuse. Meanwhile they should have been arrested and sent to the state penitentiary.

Therefore, I know first hand, we need state prisons, and they have their place in society. However, prison should not be a place where white correction officers ridicules, torture, starve and treat minorities as they are terrorist slaves, making them suffer as though they are in Guantanamo Bay, and minority Correction Officers go along to fit in.

Well that's what happens in state prisons, and if you think for one moment it can not happen to you or your loved one, think again. We are all guilty of believing those prison series we see on TV, they must have done something wrong if they are in jail. Well I am telling you that is bullshit. I strongly believe 50% of the state inmates are innocent, just indigent. In order to fight a case, you need money, not proof.

It is important you pay close attention to this chapter because state prison is 100 times worst than Rikers Island and it sets us back 100 years. The sad part is no one cares or listens to the pleas and cries from inmates and their family member regarding the harsh treatment they are receiving by the guards. Society has written them off like bad apples, until it hits close to home.

New York State Correctional facilities, often referred to as the state pens, penitentiary, up north, the mountains, jail , prison, concentration camps and Guantanamo Bay. Unlike Rikers Island, the state guards carry batons; heavy beige batons, and they will crack you upside your head in a nano second.

The difference between a Rikers Island/County jails and NYS Correctional prison inmates is; accused and convicted. Accused you reside on Rikers/County jail. Convicted you reside in a state prison in the mountains.

It is alleged, the further you go up into the Mountains, the more ruthless, sadistic, abusive and racist, the Correction Officers become. They control the jails and will literally break your neck, and get away with murder, and allegedly, have in the past.

Allegedly, these state facilities have dungeons where they take inmates and you never hear from them again.

Each state prison has a goon squad and secret society. The New York State prisons secret society guards are allegedly identified by the Mohawk haircut. Whereas hair is shaved off both the sides of their heads. They are allegedly kkk racist, lack a conscience and stick together regardless, and will never rat another officer out. It's alleged that a guard who rats out one of their own, can wind up dead in the dumpster and an inmate will take the weight for this uncommitted crime

They do not give a damn about the inspector general, police, Albany, Attorney General, FBI, CIA or the President. They do what they want and answer to nobody but the Commissioner. They allegedly have the green light and protection of the almighty Governor and Correction Commissioner.

"How they get away with attempted murder on an inmate"

How to get away with attempted murder on an inmate. This is how the correction officers will damn near kill an inmate over a personal testosterone ego crisis, shift blame , cover it up with the assistance of their supervisors and get away with it. I saw first hand how they get away with attempted murder on an inmate. I will give you a systematic account on how they carry out this act of official misconduct.

The first thing I hear a person states is "I'll call Albany" Well sweetie pie call on because they could care less. As long as it is officer on inmate. The officer is always right. They may act like they are entertaining your complaint, but all they do is notify the person you are complaining about and that could possibly get your loved one in more physical danger. No matter how many complaints or how many times a person files a complaint. They sweep it under the rug and figure you will go away.

The Correction Officers at Greenhaven Correctional Facility in Stormville NY beat my nephew to a pulp on Saturday , November 29, 2014 , as the Captain watched from the sidelines. By the grace of God, he is still alive. Had I not stepped in the results might have been different.

The beating occurred at 9am in front of fifty inmates. The news of the beating spread throughout the jail like a wildfire . Concerned inmates had their family members contact me. The message I received "the CO's just jumped your nephew, get a lawyer and get up here immediately. I called the jail immediately and identified myself. I visited my nephew several days later and he did not have to tell me what happened. Twenty years as a Correction Officer has taught and conditioned me to believe nothing I hear. not even my nephew. Assess and investigate.

However, is obvious they used excessive force because he was having difficulty walking. If you look at the visit footage, you will view for yourself. Also, look at my nephew's demeanor. What I saw on that visit was a part of my nephew's soul taken. That vision still haunts me and that is my driving force for exposing state corrections.

No matter how many people I contacted, how inconsistent the guards reports, how much evidence and witnesses my nephew had in his favor, including a statement from a Correction Officer. The kangaroo court conducted by the Deputy Superintendent Collado allowed the correction officers to get away with attempted murder.

A Correction Officer can get away with excessive force/attempted murder as long as they do not have any a medical records paper trailing to contradict a beating. Yes, I refer to it as attempted murder because if an inmate beats the daylights out of them, utilizing the same tactics. Attempted murder is what they will be charged with in a court of law. .

Another tactic they use is to beat the inmate away from the institutional cameras and focus on his body only, no facial bruises. They resort to threatening him with more bodily harm (via baton) to sign a medical refusal form in front of a physician.

Just in case, they think the inmate's injuries may be problematic in the future. They will state the inmate either bit them or blackened their eye. The latter is extreme, but if the injuries are near death, they will resort to either a colleague or self- inflicted injuries, in this sick act.

In my nephew's case, the guard stated my nephew bit him. While in the clinic, the goon guards, placed him in a chokehold him with the batons and made him take an AIDS test, to cover their tracks. I know you are scratching your head saying "what the hell an AIDS test have to do with anything. I will give you the inside scoop on the correction officers playbook.

If a correction officer uses excessive force on an inmate, its major paperwork.   Unjustifiable force can create problems for the administration. An inmate can sue and bring unwanted attention to that institution. Therefore, they must cover their asses. I was informed that one of the superior officers on duty that day was informed by an inmate they were beating my nephew up in the hallway and he should investigate. He walked over to the area and clearly stated out loud "What the hell are you doing ? I want no part of this. Clean this shit up. Therefore, the correction officer has to say my nephew assaulted him first. The report the guard wrote was a joke. This particular officer said my nephew just walked over to him and punched him in the face.

COVER UP - 101

After the incident he makes my nephew refuse medical attention and with the next breath makes him take an AIDS test by submitting blood. The refusal of medical attention is; so the injuries are not documented. An inmate cannot prove they were beat up is there are no documents / evidence to back it up. It becomes hearsay. The guards will threaten and do whatever is necessary to deter an inmate from being examined by a physician. The AIDS test is to enable the guard to cover their asses if an investigation ensues in the future. Not only is he falsifying documents. (federal crime) He is violating an inmate's civil right by forcing him to submit to a blood test for AIDS. (federal crime)

Common sense is all you need to figure out something is fishy. There are two reasons why I knew this was bullshit.

Number one; my nephew hates needles. Number two; why would my nephew refuse medical attention for himself ; he was bloodied and couldn't walk, they had to carry him into the clinic.

On the other hand volunteer to let them stick a needle in his arm to help the correction officer , who just beat him up; to prove his case, that my nephew bit him so he had to use excessive force. Red flags, red flags, red flags.

Meanwhile no evidence of the officer's bite marks via pictures. At the hearing, the deputy superintendent shows a picture of a hand to my nephew, just a hand, and no other body parts attached, no medical records for the guard to prove injuries. No proof of a tetanus shot, no district attorney re-arrest

This is a page out of the ole correction officer's playbook. The correction officers lie, their supervisor conducts the hearing . Of course, the inmate is found guilty. I've seen it too many times. My nephew was found guilty, privileges revoked and sent to solitary confinement for 1 year, with "Assault on Officer" fiagged on his locater card. That means open- season for any institution he resides at. When Correction Officers see that notation, they may randomly beat you down. Another one bites the dust. Covered up with the blessings of the Commissioner and Governor. The reason I state with their blessings, is because at the end of the day. They are responsible for the correctional facilities, whether they blatantly co-sign or not.

***If the beating is too severe. They will move the inmate from jail to jail , so his family cannot find him.

STATE PRISON LIFE

Let us get down to the nitty gritty about state prison. Contrary to what you might have heard or believe. State prison is not a country club; inmates do not have it made in prison. All prisons are a negative environment and a reflection of the streets; especially in urban America. When you put people in a cage with nothing to do, eventually they will retort to the temperament of the environment.

The same thing applies to a Correction Officer. Correction Officers need be careful or they take on the mannerisms of an inmate. They do not see it or realize it, but everyone around them can see the difference.

Unbelievably state prison is big business for inmates and Correction Officers. Drugs and weapons sold at high prices and there is a lot of money made in prison. The state guards are paid less than city guards which I think is ridicules they are dealing with lifers with nothing to lose. Pay them more and the reported and unreported corruption and conditions at the prisons may decline. It would be more tempting for a state correction officer to compromise their position because their salaries are damn near at the poverty line. Pay them more and they have something to lose. Nobody wants to give up a good paying job. The ranking officers recognize this. That is why they will instruct a guard to do their dirty work and sell them down the river need be.

NO SNITCH POLICY

Every jail or prison has a no snitch policy. There is an unwritten code in any state prison. No snitching allowed for correction officers or inmates. In city prisons, if a correction officer snitches they will be tormented by their colleagues. In state, prison a snitching guard's body, may be discovered floating in a river or dumpster . In a state facility, an inmate will never tell authorities about drug or weapon activity because they will have to deal with guards and inmates.

If you complain to Albany or a higher authority. They will make your life a living hell. They will destroy your legal work, tear up your incoming mail and illegally read your outgoing mail. Of course they won't admit it. They will also pay an inmate to beat your ass and plant a weapon in your cell. You cannot snitch under any circumstances. I know my nephew follows that unwritten policy. Greenhaven was an exception because he never complains. His sentiment has always been; I want to focus on getting my wrongful conviction overturned and going home.

WHAT TO EXPECT

What should you expect if you are a new inmate entering state prison? For starter you can expect to be challenged or a beat down by the other inmates, especially if you have no street credibility or don't know a bunch of people in jail. Your life will literally be a living hell. They will take by force, your sneakers , commissary and whatever else they can get their hands on. Most of the time the guards will look the other way. Now that is just with your peers, at some point, you will experience the wrath of the angry and racist correction officers. You will hear a bunch of slavery derogatory terms such as nigger, coon, spic, and chink bastard etc. Their main slogan is; "what you looking at boy I will bury you, dig you up, and bury you again boy". You will see guards constantly tell an inmate to face the wall, if they think they were talking in the corridor. At some point they might bash their faces into the concrete wall for just turning around for fear about what the guard is about to do to them. On a regular basis you will see guards perform gang style beating on inmates, while all the other inmates remain silent. Do not expect the holiday inn.

The public thinks they get three hots (meal) and a cot (bed). The cot is about 2 inches thick and uncomfortable   The three hots are soy meals on a tray that is sufficient to feed a 5 year old. One small tray that leaves an inmate hungrier than before they ate.   Meat has been primarily eliminated from the male prison menus. The female prisoners fought to get meat back on the menu. Feeding them small tiny pieces of chicken calling the meal chicken ala king is ludicrous. Everything is soy and I think that is deliberate by the state. You want to weaken the inmate

Oh I see what is going on. A muscular built inmate is a threat. They do not want these inmates to bulk up anymore. They prefer them weak and frail. That is why you barely see inmates all muscled up. Not unless their family is sending packages and money on a regular basis. Long gone are the days whereas the inmates come home all muscle bound bulked up.

They are literally starving the inmate. I am not saying they should eat gourmet meals. However, we are not Ethiopia and starving an inmate is cruel and inhumane can make a person mentally unstable. There is nothing worse than being hungry.

The public also thinks inmates get jobs and make money in jail. That is a myth. There are a handful of jobs in prison. They cut all the funding because no one cares about you once you go to jail and they sure do not want to spend any money on you. You can expect to be treated like a second-class citizen and tormented on a daily basis. Your visitors will be disrespected, and talked down on, as though they are the ones incarcerated, to discourage them from visiting in the future. It may take anywhere from 10-30 days to receive mail and or a package from your loved ones.

WHERE DO WE GO FROM HERE

I will tell you where we go from here. The unwarranted excessive racial gang style use of force has to stop. These inmates are not slaves, and when you treat them as such, you set the country back centuries .The media and justice department has to get involved. The governor need to institute a bill of rights for inmates like Mayor Deblasio did here in New York City , if there is not one in place. If there is one in place, the justice department needs to monitor it. The justice department has to place undercover inmates , correction and ranking officers in the jails.

The family members need to band together and overflow the justice department and social media with every act of violence these correction officers inflict on inmates. They need to file lawsuits. The day of nobody cares and they are not going to do, anything is long gone. You have to make them do something, by becoming a thorn in their sides. Social media saw to that. If you stay on their asses and keep exposing them, trust me in the long run they will think twice before committing gang style beatings on inmates.   If someone does not step in, the blood of dead correction officers will be on their hands as well.

There's a new generation of inmates and they are not kum-ba-yah as the inmates were in the past. You abused and beat down most of these inmates' parents and in turn. They inflicted that same type of behavior to their kids. I guarantee you if you research many of these prisoners background their fathers/mother's were incarcerated Or their father's were just absent. These inmates are in reality, tired of being hammered and eventually are going to snap and murder these correction officer's for laying their paws on them. Physical and mental pain on any individual, eventually takes its toll .

How is Governor Cuomo going to explain, a guard, killed in the jail in the line of duty, in prison? You cannot turn your focus immediately to other inmates like those that you allegedly did with the Clinton escape. Your response cannot be placing more correction officer's lives in jeopardy by giving the green light to go in and damn near kill inmates. When in fact with the mounds of letters of complaints sitting on the Governor's desk that he chose to ignore ; he is responsible and has been turning a blind eye to the abuse of power in state prisons since his term started. (I give kudos to Mayor DeBlasio; at least he's trying to address the Rikers Island problems)

Riots will ensue and more blood will be Governor Cuomo's hands. I cannot speak about any jail but Greenhaven Correctional Facility, because my nephew never had a problem with any officers at the other institutions. At least he has not told me about. The only thing I keep hearing out of his mouth is they don't care. The guards do not care. Every time I hear that irks me. However, if what happened to my nephew seems similar, then it needs to be reported.

Furthermore, find something for these inmates to do. Make them work eight hours a day. You cannot expect them to sit in their cells all day and be calm and productive. Give them jobs. Make them clean, paint, cook, take courses, build etc. Those cells should be empty for the most part during the day and they should be mentally occupied working.. Make them work a 40-hour week. That is the American way and put the money back in the jails. This should pay for programs, food, supplies, etc.

CHAPTER 16

THE ELEPHANT IN THE ROOM

This is the part of the book that some of my colleagues , looking to discredit me, have been flipping the pages, driving themselves crazy, to see if I included in my memoirs. They want to see if I revealed my connection with this high- powered individual. There are several reasons why I must reveal this relationship in this book .

My primary reason one is, I will not let my colleagues define my association and relationship with this person, whom I had a great deal of respect for and try to paint me as a whore.

Furthermore, I do not want to sit on a talk show or interview and the host either reveals my association with this individual, or my former colleagues will call in and try to put me on blast because, it is common knowledge.

I will cut to the chase and reveal the elephant in the room. In 1984, I had a brief intimate relationship with none other than Eric M Taylor. Yes, he retired as the New York City Correction Chief of Operations and yes they named a building after him the "Eric M Taylor Center".

What people do not know is the intimate aspect lasted about three months and the friendship was intact up until a couple of years ago. I haven't spoken to him in years and assume I never will again, after the release of this book.

The reason I have to address this is that in the beginning, I specifically told him not to tell anyone because he was married and we weren't going to last. However, just like any man would do; he instituted bragging rights. It appears the whole world knew and it wasn't glorious.

The relationship would haunt me for the rest of my career. That is why I completely understand what Correction Officer Tomara Bryan's went through and why she filed a lawsuit. My relationship with Eric Taylor subjected me to physical, verbal and emotional abuse, throughout my entire career.

When I met him, I was still a rookie officer in NYCCIFM (C-76) and he was a provisional Assistant Deputy Warden there. Our first encounter was on a midnight tour and for me comical; probably ballsy on my part to him. He was making his rounds throughout the jail and the phone were ringing and everyone was getting there act together. "Walking" and "Dep Walking' chants were throughout the building. The Correction Officers were getting updating their log and memo books because the tour commander was making his rounds, throughout the jail.

I was working the "A" station in the housing area at the time. All of a sudden I hear "on the gate". I came from inside the "A" station and this short black handsome with a crispy white shirt was standing there. I laughed so hard as I opened the gate to let him in, he asked me what was so funny. I stated "All of this ruckus, for you". That is how we met. I was always a straight shooter and spoke my mind.

I do not remember how it escalated to the next level. I do remember that when it did, I told him specifically not to tell anyone. He was married, his wife pregnant and I knew it was wrong. Looking back now I realized I was kind of lonely and vulnerable. I had just broken up with the love of my life; my childhood sweetheart.

Eric was a great distraction. In addition, he was so cool. He never acted like a vulture like most of my male colleagues. I was extremely fascinated with his intellect, how smart and goal driven he was. It does not surprise me decades later, he climbed the ranks to hold the prestigious title of Chief of Operations. That was only one rank shy of Commissioner.

Contrary to what people believe there were no hotels, late night dinners, gifts, payment for sex, promises of I love you I am going to leave my wife, no special office positions, no office hoe downs, no disrespect , no boasting on my part and absolutely no oral sex. (I figured I would throw that in) He did not buy my houses, cars and pay for my expensive trips around the world. That is why I went to work everyday; to support myself. Even at that age I was not looking for a man to be my savior or take care of me. I was an independent woman and did not need a man to validate me.

Eric lived in Long Island, but would visit me at my apartment at 512 Stone Avenue, in the Brownsville Houses in Brooklyn NY, in the housing projects. We had a couple of intimate encounters. Nevertheless, I was not in love with him and it was not primarily a sexual relationship and in fact I was the one who ended the relationship. I told him to take a hike approximately three months later because he stood me up three times too many.

As much as people would like to insinuate my relationship with him was because he was a ranking officer. As far as I was concerned; he was a just man and I do not care who you are. You do not stand me up. I realize now, if he did not have respect for me, he could have made my life a living hell. After I told him to lose my number and cut him off I went on to meet my future husband.

Several years later, he saw me at my husband's graduation ceremony. Yes, I said husband., I moved on with life and got married. Eric and I reconnected as friends

I divorced my husband had a baby thereafter, left the job from 1991 -1994 (child care leave). Upon returning back to work. Realizing I was a single parent and needed stabile work hours. I contacted Eric because I needed steady hours to take care of my little girl. He was just promoted to Chief of Operations and transferred me to Brooklyn Court Division.

As soon as I returned to work. I learned he called Brooklyn Courts and told them my woman is coming down there, take care of her. I was fuming. I was trying to start new and now I was once again "ERIC'S BITCH". I called him up very upset and asked him why he said that. He had no idea what I went through in my career because of him.

I believe to a certain degree, my affiliation with Eric Taylor created a lot of havoc. You would think my connection to such a powerful man, people would back off. To be quite blunt. The white people did and the black people acted a damn fool. I think a lot of the resentment and back-stabbing from my black female colleagues, stemmed from the jealousy of my relationship with Eric.

I had a bull's-eye on my back my entire career. Eric Taylor has no idea how much anxiety and stress, I had to endure my entire career and post retirement because in the minds of many, I will forever be connected to him as his lover.

We were friends. His daughter was an actress in one of my movies. I was also his invited guest to the ribbon cutting of Eric M Taylor Center on Rikers Island.

I do not regret my friendship with him. I do however regret having a brief sexual relationship with him. He was a married man and my boss. It's a regret I cannot undo.

CHAPTER 17

THERE IS HOPE LET'S FIX IT

Yes, I believe there is hope and we can fix this broken system. It is not going to be simple; this has been years in the making and there is a deep-seated culture of violence that has been growing like a cancer throughout the years.

For starters, the correction officer mindset has to change; slavery days are over and the USA is not a dictatorship country. We need to be honest and acknowledge there is a major problem. The media has done a great job here in New York City exposing corrupted correction officers and abuse of inmates. The NYC Mayor and Commissioner have partly recognized there is a problem as well, regarding corruption and inmate abuse; but has backtracked on certain issues. Correction Officers need to stop blaming Mayor De Blasio and Commissioner Ponte. They just got here. I didn't hear all this noise when Bloomberg or Guiliani were in charge.

The public's biased misconception about incarceration needs altering. We are all guilty of turning our noses up to and judging anyone who is in prison or has gone to prison. It is an easy assumption when you get your facts from a reality TV shows. I used to be guilty of that until I began working there.

Society needs to be deprogrammed and sensitized. If your first impression of a person incarcerated is cynical and you do not flinch at the notion that guards are overly abusing inmates, and assume they deserve it, this applies to you. Keep in mind. Rikers Island prisoners have only been accused, not convicted. Stop making them a bad guy before they had a chance to have their day in court.

Prison abuse is not limited to inmates. No one has mentioned the physical and mental abuse female correction officers are suffering at the hands of their male colleagues: I know personally I have since learned of other cases and these female officers' cries have gone unheard.

In order to begin to fix this mess you have to address the major problem with male correction officers and their overuse of testosterone in city and state corrections. The majority of assault cases are involving male guards and male inmates.

Prison life is not text book and in order to understand Rikers Island; you have to be in the trenches. You cannot possibly understand what either goes through on a daily basis. If it were an easy environment, everyone would sign up for it.

With that being said; New York State corrections are a different story and they play by a different set of rules, and there needs an intense steady spotlight on the hidden corruption and murderous abuse that has plagued the prison system for decades. Rampant unjustified brutalization against inmates is common. If a correction officer is charged with excessive force, against an inmate, and I say IF, because nine times out of ten the guard will get away with it. Most likely, the judicial system will fail because the trial will be filled with a jury of their peers that will always favor the guards, especially in the mountains. The settings for these jails are in a small town that relies on the prisons to support their communities. Many guards live in these small towns and are kin to the potential jury members if the case goes to trial. Therefore whereas state corrections is concerned. All trials need a change of venue and that should be New York City. Yes, it seems far fetched, but a fair trial might ensue and the facts will be looked at versus the family member looking out for the abusive guards.

Correction Officers know exactly what is going on and need to come from behind the blue wall, admit and expose their dishonest and violent colleagues because they are creating a hostile and unsafe environment for their fellow officers, as well.

Correction Officers job description is care, custody and control. That is it, point-blank. Yes, it is a dangerous job. We do not have a problem accepting the check every two weeks. Therefore, we should perform the duties for which hired to do. We were not hired to kiss their asses and take them to recitals and dance class. That is not what I am insinuating. If we could stick to the basic script, that might alleviate unnecessary tragedy and distribution of our taxpaying dollars to pay lawsuits.

The Correction academy needs to stop brainwashing correction officer's into believing we are at war. If you train a new recruit that prisoners are Guantanamo Bayish characters, of course they will approach inmates in a war-like manner and automatically be on the defensive. They are only following the rules in place. They need high quality sensitivity training.

A correction officer sounds less than smart and biased, when defending our former commissioner Bernard Kerik, who violated the law and went to prison for committing multiple crimes. Praises and kind words were displayed. However, Rikers Island is full of prisoners who have, only been, accused of a crime, not convicted and labeled everything but the child of God. That needs to change; the level of unwarranted disrespect I have viewed in my career is overwhelming.

Let us begin the fixing process. In order to stop the mental and physical abuse and excessive force inflicted upon inmates; covert hidden cameras, with sound, need to he installed in every institution and monitored by the justice department. No one should know where the cameras are; but the justice department. Not even the Wardens or Superintendents, Commissioners, Mayors or Governors; they are part of the problem too.

It is easy for correction officers to behave correctly when they know the cameras are watching them, or take them to the blind spots and beat them down. However, if they do not know where the cameras are they will try a different method of communication. Not necessarily hug a thug, but definitely not calling them coons, niggers, spics , boy or asshole..

All of the jail's assault on officer's records needs extensive investigating by the justice department, in particular facilities like Greenhaven State Correctional Facility, because that is the facility inmates beg to transfer there to be closer to their families. That is where most of the assaults on guards, are transpiring. If there are so many assaults on Correction Officers, why is that? The Justice Department needs to comb through all the paperwork and reinvestigate each case.

If a Correction Officer is involved in so many assault attempts on them. The problem is probably the correction officer. Stevie Wonder can see that

All of the inspector general employees need to be re-trained, rerouted and possibly fired. Send all Inspector General employees back the jails if they were hired to be a correction officer, no Correction Officer should be working in the inspector general office. It is definitely a conflict of interest and many do not know how to be impartial; they automatically side with the correction officer.

Each inspector general officer should be assigned, to a jail or prison and they should be fully responsible if there is consistent corruption at their assigned jail and it was not dealt with.

How will they know its consistent corruption? They will know because there will be a hotline and physical address for inmates and correction officers to report wrongdoing. At that point, an undercover inspector general transfers into that institution as an inmate to investigate the targeted area. Once they get confirmation, they will transfer the undercover out. This is not far fetched. The police departments have many undercover units. They have cops posing as bloods crypts and thugs. If they want corruption to end, they need to invest the money.

In addition, abusive officers need to undergo random psychological tests to be conducted by the justice department, especially after excessive physical force has been used in numerous occasions. Correction Officers views change after they have been there for a while. Just like random drug test, they need random psychological test.

Background checks need to be more extensive. An outside agency from another city should handle the hiring process, not active Correction Officers. There are too many hookups. It is the; who you know, who you blow , your people call my people syndrome. I should know better than anyone, I got my sister hired, with one phone call.

Correction Officers need to go for sensitivity communication classes every three months as part of their training. Their attitudes are the worst in law enforcement. You might say police officers attitudes are the worst. I say no, they do not say much they will just shoot and kill you.

The facilities that house adolescents need to have all sorts of programs, they need to find something for them to do. They have a lot of energy to burn. They are kids and kids are active. If you have them sitting them in the dorms and housing areas all day; what do you expect. They are going to wild out. Most of these kids have issues and most likely it is with their parents. Many of their parents have failed them no matter which way you look at it. It might not have been intentional, but it exists. They need counseling, psychiatric care , education and to learn a skilled trade. If they are a known leader of the gang, remove them from the housing area and place them around people who are not in gangs and monitor their behavior. If you remove the gang president and gang vice president and separate the two, the gang gets weaker, then monitor their phone calls and you can see their next course of action.

Each housing area has a leader and that leader can make or break the difference.

I already spoke about mental health and my solution to handling the mental health inmates is to hire people with a degree in mental health. Train them as a correction officer and pay them extra.

Solitary Confinement should be eliminated period - point blank.

You cannot close Rikers Island. It's not the building. It's the people who need to be fixed. Closing Rikers Island and transferring the same abusive and corrupt correction officers, is defeating the purpose. Besides that:

where do you put all the prisoners. Eventually some of them will be found guilty.

Now you say; how are we going to pay for this. First close those state solitary confinement facilities that were newly opened in rural areas to enrich the communities, or for the sake of the homies in private industry making a quick buck. That is a ton of money there.

In the state facilities get rid of all those nasty ass soy bagged food products you are serving the inmates; because once again, the homies got the private industry contracts to solicit that garbage you are feeding the inmates in state prisons. (You would not eat it or let your dog eat it)

Now do not get me wrong, I am not saying state inmates should get gourmet meals but these grown ass men are starving in state prison. I know that nasty ass food is expensive. It's my tax paying dollars and getting dumped in the garbage because the state inmates can't stomach it on many occasions, no matter how hungry they are. They stress out their families for packages or money for commissary to get decent food to eat.

They deliver the food in giant bags, pre-cooked, dump it in a big pot and serve them in a tray fit for a five year old. That is pure hatred and torture.

If they want to leave the menu as is. Make the guards eat it too. Do not allow them to bring in food from the outside. Better yet; I challenge Governor Cuomo and Acting Commissioner Annucci to eat at any state prison they supervise for one week. I do not know about now, but Rikers Island food is even better than that. Change the menu especially since my alternative is to put everyone to work.

There is a new system in place: designated television jails and package jails. If you are housed in a TV jail. You cannot receive a monthly package.

If you are housed at a package jail. You cannot have a TV in your cell to occupy your mind. Excuse my French, but " What kind of shit is that ? " . Its either eat and no TV or don't eat and watch TV.

Every single inmate should be getting up at the crack of dawn, like everyone else and working. They could not work in the streets; let them work in the jails. Let them grow and cook the food. Let them raise the chickens and cows. Everything that is needed in the jails let them make it. Not just a couple of jails; all of the upstate prisons.

Let us bring back "MADE IN AMERICA" all the way. Not just a couple of items here or there.. This will be the opportunity for America to be back on the map and the outsourcing to China can end. I know the prisons already have inmate-making products. However, inmates should make everything that the prisons use. The prison system can make money by selling the products the state inmates make. No one has to know they made it either. I offer a lot more solutions but will save some for my speaking engagements.

Stop withholding the inmate's mail for two to three weeks, from their loved ones. Outside communication is needed. It can make or break a difference in an officer's tour of duty.

If we tackle and weed out the bad abusive and corrupt officers, we may stand a chance with this new breed of inmates flooding the system in the last decade. If we do not I can guarantee you a riot is brewing.

No matter how hard you try to stop the inmate movement of justice they are forming in every jail.They are getting more powerful and resistant to the bully tactics. Eventually a couple of riots will ensue and innocent officers and inmates will be killed. Yes murdered in the line of duty. That blood will be on the administrations hands for turning a blind eye or condoning this behavior.

For many years, correction officers have known some of their ranking officers to be part of the weapon and drug pushers of the jails. Many have already retired. My question is who took their places. Get rid of the abuse and drugs

They need to bring in the weapons and drug-sniffing dogs into housing and cell areas and correction and ranking officers locker rooms on a regular random basis. There is too much drugs and the inmate's visitors are not the only ones bringing it in. I would say ion drug scan the correction officers as well as the inmates, but I believe that process is faulty. There is hope and this broken system can be fixed now. .

OPEN LETTER TO PRESIDENT OBAMA

I know many people are probably wondering why I am penning a letter to the President. There are several reasons why.

Number one; you are responsible for the entire United States of America. Number two; you lived in New York City, and know first hand about the prejudices in the New York judicial system. By the grace of God, you did not fall in the cracks. This is not my first time reaching out to you. I have been reaching out to you about my nephew Delamar Brown, since you were a candidate for your first term to become the President of the United States. I know you taught constitutional law and my nephew's rights were being violated during his each trial and I was praying you would help. He had 3 trial in one year and was subjected to a whole lot of prosecutorial misconduct. The only thing I was requesting was a fair trial. I guess that was wishful thinking. www.delamarbrown.com

I recently contacted you regarding my nephew because he was beat to a pulp by the Correction Officers in Greenhaven Correctional facility and they were breaking the law by falsifying documents to cover up their actions. If you read the chapter on "New York State Greenhaven Thugs "you will see the letter I wrote to you.

I am respectfully requesting you send a watchdog team into that facility and get interrogatories from every inmate in that facility as well as comb the records on assaults on officers in that facility. Also, compare that with, how many cases the district attorney prosecuted. You will uncover just how corrupt this facility is. It has to stop. No one is paying attention to state facilities. Yes 50% may be guilty and a large portion may be lifers. Nevertheless, It's our taxpaying dollars that are paying these lawsuits and the torture some of them are enduring: you might as well put them in front of a firing squad and shoot them.

Some of these correction officers are dismantling these grown ass men for no reason at all, there are no consequences and Albany is ignoring their please for help. Let these inmates upstate do their time.

What I will say is: these inmates are our age, and you and I lived in New York City in the 80's and by the grace of God we were never arrested.

The thing that saddens me the most is, I gave my life to this correctional institution and the level of disrespect I received as an active duty and retiree, from New York City and State Corrections is unbelievable.

As a retiree my nephew was beat up by the correction officers. I step in to protect him and expose corruption and I am now a target of ion scanning ridicule every time I step in a New York State Correctional Facility. My name is flagged in Albany's master book My reputation is tarnished because of whistle blowing. If you don't believe me look at the master list for visitor and there, and my name is marked. Look how many times I was ion scanned before and after I filed complaints against Greenhaven Correctional Facility. I know you are a busy man but please look into this for me. Once this book comes out my nephew , my family and I will be retaliated against. I can almost guarantee it. Please keep an eye on us.

OPEN LETTER TO MEN IN CORRECTION

I am directing this open letter ONLY to the exceedingly antagonistic men in New York City and State correction department. Stop the avoidable cruelty. You are making the job difficult for your colleagues. Your violent actions is the one of the key reasons a negative beam is on the correction department overall. It's making the prisoners more violent and costing the taxpayers money.

Many of you come to work with your chest out, fist clenched, bullying and provoking inmates, creating a hostile toxic environment. You lack compassion and operate solely on egos

There is definitely too many alcoholics on the job. If you are abusing drugs and alcohol; get help. Your law enforcement status, equipped with drugs, alcohol and a firearm; feeds your overzealous egos.

In addition: you assume the roles of predator and sexual abuser, treating your female colleagues like a piece of prostitution whore meat.

Yes, you are physically stronger than we are but that does not give you the right to rule us. We took the same exam, receive the same training, and earn the same pay. We are entitled to respect.

You decide you want to have sex with us and try to make us comply. If we do not, you isolate and treat us as if we are yesterday's trash and will intentionally place our lives in danger. You need to realize we are your equal as well as someone mother, daughter, sister and caretaker, etc.

To the ranking officers, not every female officer is your property for the choosing. Our body parts do not belong to you. If we decline to become part of your harem, you go after our jobs and try to make our lives a living hell. Instead of focusing on; care, custody and control, your primary focus is the ego, vagina and who has the most testosterone. Oh not let me forget for many penis; is your passion too. You come to work as if you are on a hunting expedition, looking for prey. The prey is either an inmate or female officer.

Many of you have a wives home and my heart goes out to some of the women who are at home paying tribute to your loving doting significant other.

What you do not know is; while you are at home paying tribute to your correction officer male counterpart. They are fighting over female officers especially the new recruits, in addition to female inmates and male inmates. They are telling you they are doing overtime and elsewhere feeding their egos. It is no reflection on you, just insecurity within him. Some of you male officers, really need to get a grip, you are an embarrassment.

OPEN LETTER TO WOMEN IN CORRECTION

This open letter to is directed to the female colleagues , I worked with during my career. I know some of you are not going to like what I am about to state but I am going to keep it real. I can literally count on one hand the female officers who never gave me a problem.

"My Hell as a Rikers Guard" this is primarily based upon my experiences with what my Black and West Indian female officers put me through from the first day on the job to the last day on the job.

Some of you are the most hateful mean spirited individuals I have ever encountered in my life. You spent the majority of your days gossiping, fighting, lying, cursing and eating your careers away. I watched every other race stick together and bond and we try to tear each other down.

You never took into account I had a life outside of corrections and a little girl to take care of. You tried to get me fired or transferred because???? I still don't know.

People have said you felt threatened by me or were jealous of me. Why? I didn't bother anyone and all I wanted to do was go to work, do my job and go home.

I don't believe you felt threatened or was jealous. Accessing it now; I think there were some underlying insecure issues, that had nothing to do with me.

To the females who are presently on the job: If a female colleague tries to trip you down a flight of the locker room stairs. File a police report to prevent that female colleague of further harming you or any other female colleague. Otherwise they will undeservingly climb the ranks, like the one who tried to trip me down the stairs, when I was a rookie officer.

If a female officer curses you, out in front of inmates, court officers and your colleagues. Write her ass up and make them send her for a psyche evaluation. That is not normal behavior.

If a clique of females write bitch on your locker on your days off. Get a magic marker, put Miss in from of the bitch, and write a thank you at the end

Stop! the backstabbing, petty jealousy, gossiping, fighting, bullying, setting up and lying on each other.

If you feel, they have you on the burn, by putting you in all the undesirable post, to work. Do not fret. Pat your self on the back, because that only means; your knee will be intact when you retire.

Please, Please Stop! being a doorknob letting your male colleagues take turns on you. For many you are just a notch; they do not want to wife you.

Stop! the jail prostitution; the scam of sleeping with ranking officers just so you can take them to court for child support and double your salary, or get an easy inmate free assignment, is a trifling.

Stop! talking about your colleagues to the inmates that means you are too comfortable and next thing you know you will be in the shower or officer's bathroom having sex with them.

Please Stop! sleeping with inmates and stop being their illegal narcotics and weapons mules. These inmates do not give a damn about you. These inmates are not cute or you bae, or boo. If you are that insecure, go seek counseling to figure out why you falling for the oldest inmate trick in the book.

Stop! coming to work with an attitude and taking it out on your colleagues and definitely stop taking it out on the inmates. If they ask you for the minimum standards things they are entitled to. Do you job! If an inmate ask you for toilet paper "Get the fuck outta my face, don't ask me for shit "is not the proper response. You will get your teeth knocked out. Fair enough, that inmate will get in trouble, but now you will spend the rest of your life with false teeth.

If you do not like working with inmates, and cannot function without an attitude. Quit ! This job is not for you

Please focus on care-custody–control and reform. Let this job be a financial stepping-stone to greater things.

LETTER TO FAMILIES OF THE INCARCERATED

I think it is very important to address the families of anyone incarcerated especially the mothers, fathers or primary caretaker. As a Correction Officer, I have always looked at each and every prisoner, regardless of age as someone's child. No child on this earth asked to be born. It is your responsibility to try to rear them correctly. Yes, many times we fall short because our upbringing lacked in many areas. Many of those instances are children suffer and possibly act out. After a certain point there is nothing we can do but pray and support them from the sidelines, not turn your back on them or wash your hands of them. You have to see your child through to the grave. That is what you signed on for when you have children. .

There are countless inmates in city and state prisons, whose family has totally turned their backs on them and I think it is disheartening. I am speaking from experience.

Rikers Island is within city limits and easy to get to via public transportation. However, if they are incarcerated in a New York State prison yes it is a distance. I understand many cannot afford to travel far away. Therefore it leaves many inmates alone and vilnerable, it can be detrimental to their well being physically , mentally and emotionally.

Therefore, some State Correction Officers prey on and pay close attention to those inmates who lack family member support. They are easy targets for slave plantation behavior often cherished by some of these sadistic state and city correction officers.

A stamp is less than a dollar. To put the phone on so they can accept calls is only $25 and a bus ride there is only $50-$60. Many of you blow that at the club.

If you are visiting Olive Gardens, Red Lobster, Chinese Restaurant, Dominos, Joe's Crab Shack , Mc Donald's or eating out for lunch everyday. How do you sleep well at night knowing your family member is in jail starving because the state decides your loved ones are not worth an adult portion size meal? No, they are not celebrating in jail. They are literally starving and every time I visit my nephew in the state prison I see the vending machine emptied before the visit is over. No food is thrown away. These grown ass men are starving. LITERALLY !

To family members outside of the immediate family I say this to you: holla at your cousin or uncle or anyone who is in jail. Pay them a visit, write a letter, and send a card, even if they are not receptive to it, make that connection.

Please let your presence known. It sends a clear message and maybe an overzealous abusive Correction Officer will think twice before they try to kill your family member. Trust me there are unreported inmate deaths and horrific injuries occurring at many jails. I have heard cases whereas inmates allegedly thrown down the metal staircases resulting in broken limbs and eye extracted from their sockets. Read the article on Attica State prison whereas the inmate sued and the officers were arrested and fired. This is real. You have no idea what these inmates go through for absolutely no reason.

By now, you know I have a nephew incarcerated in a New York State prison and it saddens me to say that the only people from my family that has visited him were (wife, mother-in law-daughter-my daughter & me). Both of his parents are deceased. My father is sick , lives in another state and his wife forbids him from sending money. (maybe $25 a year) No one in my large family has visited , wrote a letter or even sent a bar of soap and he has been in jail for 10 years already. That speaks volumes to me and is sad.

Whether you believe the family member is innocent, or not inmate, they are blood relatives. The crazy part is; if that family member was famous, had money or was released from prison and was awarded a substantial sum of money, some of you out there would attempt to unite with them.

It is time to care and not throw your family under the permanent bus. Keep the line of communication open, so if something happens. They have someone to reach out. What if the shoe was on the other foot? Oh, you think you can never go to jail. Think again. I did a whole chapter on it. How would you feel if everyone abandoned you? Connect with your family member today .

I am about to start an organization to target the corruption, abuse and assist families with travel to visit their loved ones in these state facilities.

I want to build a support system to tackle this systematic abuse. New York City has close to 8.5 million people and I want to build a solid non-violent force to address the issues. Equipped with attorneys, social media and computer geeks.

I want a 24 hour hotline for inmates to call when they have been brutally beaten.

www.thedbrownproject.com

OPEN LETTER TO THE MAYOR DEBLASIO

To a certain degree, my heart goes out to you Mayor DeBlasio. I do not personally know you and I don't have a problem with the way you are handling the correction department. You are the only Mayor I've seen step to the plate on Rikers Island abuse and corruption and admit some fault and my colleagues are trying to rip you to shreds. Like its your fault the correction department is a hot mess. This was years in the making.

Unfortunately, you are the Mayor of a nasty, dirty, disgusting, struggling New York City and corrupt prison system. People expect you to walk on water and clean up this messy city, pronto. Same as they did President Obama.

It is my opinion you are being subjected to a certain level of disrespect from many people because you have a black family. They look at your dark skinned wife and son with the afro. It's called racism.

Rikers Island is a hot mess. Today's Correction Officers are paying for the sins of their predecessors. You cannot blame all of the Correction Officers. There are many first-rate ones, literally putting their lives on the line everyday. It's a very difficult job dealing with prisoners when you have no weapons or immediate back up.

You have never been a Correction Officer ort incarcerated, therefore you cannot possibly understand. I challenge you to come to Rikers Island for two days a month and work inside the worst jails, in the dorms, surrounded by prisoners all day.

Put on a uniform and do our job for 8 hours, twice a month. I guarantee you , you will have a different opinion. Hold a town hall meeting with correction officers only and no ranking officers. Just you and them. Let them tell you what they go through and direct you to the most undesirable housing areas, outside of punitive segregation.

You need to also plant some undercover officers throughout every jail and do not let anyone who they are, not the Wardens, Commissioners: no one. You will be surprised to see how many correction and ranking officers make the environment toxic.

If you do not weed out the bad officers, I am afraid you will be the first Mayor to have a Correction Officer die in the line of duty at the hands of a prisoner. If that happens, your back will be against the wall. They will blame you.

Keep in mind. Ninety percent of prisoners on Rikers Island have only been accused, of a crime not convicted. They are two-steps from civilian status.

There need to be consequences for the excessive actions by police and correction officers. Not a spa day

OPEN LETTER TO THE PRESS

I want to thank Gary Buiso from the New York Post who did the magnificent article on me and that two page spread , placed me on the map and started a chain reaction with other media outlets.http://nypost. com/2014/08/31/sex-drug-abuse-rampant-at-rikers-retired-officer/

 The New York Times has been doing some great journalism on NYS Corrections. They have contributed massive amount of abuse in New York State Prisons.

I am overall elated for the press and encouraging ALL of the press to continue to dig for the truth regarding the corruption and abuse that is widespread in the New York City prison system known as Rikers "Hells Island".

I am urging the press to embark on, major investigations starting with NYS Greenhaven Correctional Facility in Stormville, New York, just 30 minutes from the Bronx, and you will be amazed at what you will uncover and the many horrific secrets and unreported murders.

New York City jails and New York State prisons are entwined. How? Well it is like going from the frying pan into the fire. Once most inmates leave Rikers Island they either go home or to an upstate prison and the treatment get worse.

Everything you have been exposing about Rikers Island is tenfold in Greenhaven Correctional Facility. If you follow the trail, it will lead you to uncover massive physical abuse, drugs and corruption in the other New York State facilities. I will have a hotline. You are welcome to any information I obtain.

OPEN LETTER TO GOVERNOR CUOMO

When you took office, you became the Governor of all of New York State, including the less fortunate, and the inmates in all the state

First and foremost I am very disappointed in your lack of concern for my well being. I am a retired Correction Officer. I reported corruption and never heard a peep out of you. I gave my life to the correction department working among many of the male prisoners who are now custody of the state.

Your state guards beat my nephew to a pulp and my concern for his life made me a target because .

I have been subjected to humiliating regular ion scans, as though I've been smuggling a pound of weed in your state prisons. Simply because I did what I was trained to do, REPORT CORRUPTION !

Now your staff has me on Albany's master list to be scanned for drugs anytime I enter a state facility. Wow ! After I turned keys in the prisons for 20 years, I am treated like a drug smuggling convict.

Its just a matter of time before they come back with deceptive results :stating I scanned positive for drugs. I've seen and heard about those rigged test. I'm not stupid.

If my nephew turned the tables and killed or seriously injured one of your correction officers when they was trying to murder him, you would have been on every news cycle popping off the mouth about zero tolerance for inmates harming your state correction officers. The same way you were on the tube when they escaped from Clinton Correctional Facility. I cite you for failure to supervise.

I blame you for this corruption going on at Greenhaven Correctional facility and any other New York State prison . This is going on under your watch.

There is a new breed of inmates, unlike our kum-baa-yah generation. They are not going to continue to ignore the blatant hatred and abuse too many generations have accepted.   You already have one escape under your watch. What's next: a Correction Officer will die in the line of duty, in a state prison, and that Correction Officer's blood will be on your hands.

I am no longer angry, just disgusted and disappointed. I will report to the elite media and social media from here on out

OPEN LETTER TO DELAMAR BROWN

This is an open letter to you, dearest nephew. I was having difficulty writing this open letter pondering what and how to address this letter. I watched you enter this world with big eyes and a gigantic smile. There was so much hope for a great future. You were everyone's pride and joy, an exceptional and extremely smart little boy and always kind, considerate and compassionate to others. Even as a young child and now considering your circumstances, I still see those traits. Most people would have thrown in the towels with the cards you were dealt. That's why your current predicament saddens and pains my heart. You don't belong in jail.

I want to apologize because so many people have failed what was expected of them.

> 1. Your father should have sought help for his addiction, which he had under control prior to your birth and relinquished after your birth.

2. Your mother because she should have kept her eye on you, her precious gem , as she had since she carried you in her belly, not allowed herself to be enticed and lured into the world of crack-cocaine by her New York City Correction colleagues who were only looking to make a steady salary off her inevitable addiction. She should have refrained from any affiliation with these devils after work hours.

3. The 102 pct in Richmond Hill Queens, for targeting and knowingly lying on you to reach a quota and arresting you for a robbery you did not commit. Just to solve and close a case to make it look good on paper.

4. Shame on your court appointed legal aid attorney and the district attorney from Queens in charge of the case, who allowed you to sit on the Rikers plantation for 17 months, and they knew in advance the admitted criminals already confessed to the crime. It wasn't until, I gave your legal aid an ultimatum. Either they let you go or I would go to Al Sharpton and the media. Only then you were offered your freedom with a stipulation. Your freedom of time served in return for a guilty plea time, so you could not sue them for their illegal incarceration.

This brings to mind Kalief Browder who spent three years on the Rikers plantation without being convicted of a crime, while the District Attorney played possum with his life, instituting bull pen and jail cell therapy, like they do to so many prisoners on the Rikers plantation.

Had I not been a Correction Officer with ties to a high ranking officer, could you dear nephew had been a a Kalief Borwder .

Expectations continued to fall short for the District Attorney and Judge in Onedia County, Utica NY when they knowingly decided to play footsie and make a mockery of the judicial system by refusing to give you a fair trial.

They did everything from hide brady material, allowing admitted false testimony, tie the hands and movements of your attorney, in my opinion tamper with the jury pool to ensure a victory, with penning two murders on your because it was an election year and the overzealous head district attorney wanted a seat in the House of Representatives. Three trial in one year and transcripts to prove my allegations.

Expectations continued to fall short when the New York State Correction Officers in Greenhaven Correctional facility decided they wanted to attempt murder on your life by beating you to a pulp, and making you refuse medical attention, for no reason other than ego. While the house captain looked on and thereafter the deputy superintendent and superintendent denied you a fair hearing to prove misconduct and false allegations. Which resulted in punishment of a year in solitary confinement. When in fact they were the ones committing the crimes and should have been brought up on charges. Once again had I not stepped in and been quick with my pen, the abuse would have continued.

So many people have failed you as they have done to so many of the black youth. The realm of a crooked system designed to deprive the youth of meaningful life and place them on the Rikers plantation .

Racism is real and I had a front row seat through your life and observed the police officers, correction officers and Onieda County , Utica NY court system literally ruin your life and attempt to erase any hope for your future.

What I will say to you is since your birth, I have always been protective of you that has and will never change. It is my belief that in spite of what has happened to you. God will see you through this horrific ordeal and bless you with a brighter future. I will fight tooth and nail to get your sentenced overturned. There is no doubt when a legal team reads your transcripts from your 3 trials they will see how your constitutional rights were violated and you didn't get a fair trial

I apologize to you dear nephew. Every single one of us in the penal justice system have all fallen short of what was expected of us, for our own personal gain. Whether it was for our bi weekly paycheck, climbing the ladder, or political aspirations. We have and continue to fail young America.

There is no doubt in my heart, mind and soul you will be set free and God will be looking for you to dedicate your life to helping the youth and wrongfully convicted. Your aunt loves you as though you were my own son. My love for you in unconditional and I will always be by your side. I want to apologize on behalf of the judicial system

I also want to apologize for the lack of concern from our family members and all the people you helped on the outside., that have refused to acknowledge you are still alive and breathing.

I know you lost both of your parents and that must feel horrible, but know that they are with you everyday , and they do not want you to fret. Keep God close because with him all things are possible. You were born and birth is a miracle. Aunty loves you.

If anyone out there wants to reach out to my nephew just to say a couple of words of encouragement . Please do.

DELAMAR BROWN 06B2999

GREAT MEADOW CORRECTIONAL FACILITY

P.O. BOX 51

11739 STATE ROUTE 22

COMSTOCK NY 12821

OPEN LETTER TO MY BABY GIRL

I decided to write this open letter to you daughter dearest because you were probably affected the most by the torment I received from my colleagues. Why? I had to raise you and there had to be shifts in my emotional attitude throughout your entire life. Trying to raise you by myself in a healthy and loving environment while ignoring the displeasure of going to work everyday dealing with the miserable and mean spirited colleagues who's main mission was to get me fired or transferred. For no reason other than their twisted hated for me.

In spite of that, I loved you more than life itself and kept my eye on the prize. I put my all into you, and gave up my social life to focus on you. Was I a perfect mother? No. But I did my best and being a single parent was not easy.

I want to apologize to you because when I retired you were 15 years old and that's when all hell broke loose. You know; Delamar went to jail, Tee died and gramps almost died and I unknowingly had so much emotional pain to deal with and couldn't put all of my focus on you .

Life definitely through me a curve ball and I shut down and didn't get my own memo. I was walking around la-dee-da , like everything was copasetic, but now I know I was dying inside and you had to see the change in me.

I apologize for not being there more for you and we were under the same roof.. I was in the house everyday but hardly ever home.

In spite of that you took all the tools I equipped you with and took life by the balls and got your bachelor's degree. I am so proud of you and love you so much. If it wasn't for you I'd probably would have sort employment elsewhere quit my job. I would not be reaping the rewards of retirement.

When I look at you I know I did something right. I molded you to be the mini me and more. You are beautiful, smart and independent. Continue to take life by the balls and squeeze them. Get everything you want out of life . When life throws you a curve ball , Get a bat and start swinging. I love you baby girl.

Love Always

Mommy

OPEN LETTER TO THERESA T. MILLER

My dearest sister "Tee Tee" as my baby girl used to call you. I miss you terribly and wish things would have turned out differently. Your death hit me like a ton of bricks. As a matter of fact , it shut me down.

There is no bond like siblings. It's like a part of me died. We have been together all of my life, regardless of our location. Mom died and it was me and you. For the most part you watched over and protected me. Sometimes a little over protective. (lol)

Did I think you always made the best choices in life ? No, but I learned so much about life from you. You were uninhibited and real. You were a calm spirit but could turn up in a nano second to protect those who you loved. You had zero tolerance for drama and arguments. You would give a person the shirt off your back even if it was your only shirt. I see a lot of your traits in your son.

I wished I never called Eric to get you that NYC Correction Officer job. I beat myself up for many years and every now and then still have regrets.

I know its not my fault but , coulda, shoulda woulda creeps into my psyche on occasion.

I'd wish you made better choices in your life and maybe you'd still be here today. But to wish that would question my faith. I honestly believe in spite of the most horrific and painful experiences in one's life. It's all part of God's plan and when he calls you home . Your work is done here on earth.

You knew you were going home. You heard God's calling. It's ironic because I officially retired on July 1, 2005 and you came to my house that day and told me not to leave your son , who was a million miles away, about to have the fight of his life. You didn't have the strength and your heart was broken. You knew I would find the strength for what lied ahead. You died the next day ON July 2, 2005.

I know you are here watching over me and Delamar. I also know you are talking to God and together you are guiding me with this book and making sure the right people are in place for me to succeed with this message.

I know you had a hand in the New York Post article, WABC 77am Dr. Michael Savage, Nightline World News, CNN Anderson Cooper, and CNN Poppy Harlow interviews. A new writer is not privy to that type of publicity. The interview with Anderson Cooper confirmed it because it was July 2, 2015 ten years later. I told him about you but I am quite sure you know that already.

I made a promise to you to never leave your son and I won't . I didn't have to make that promise because to leave him would mean leaving you and you are a part of me. Keep looking out for us. Till we meet again. I love you.

P.S. Tell Ma I said hi and I love and miss her.

Your baby sis

Love Robin

OPEN LETTER TO SELF

I am writing this open letter to myself with the hopes that now I can close the chapter to my old life and start anew. This is my truth and no one can take if from me.

Writing this book made me realize I was going through so much emotional pain since becoming a correction officer in 1983. My core was angry, hurt and disappointed.

Throughout the years, I kept so much bottled up and acted as though everything was great because I am not one to cry over spilled milk. Meanwhile since retirement, unconsciously, I shied away from the general public and created a makeshift solitary confinement in my home. It was my safe haven. No one could bother or touch me if they couldn't see me.

No matter how I tried to pretend everything was ok, laughed, joked, la-dee-da; always a smile on my face. I was a hot mess inside and woke up one day and reality punch me in the face. Sadness and anxiety introduced themselves to me, and I turned to my almighty God for guidance and he definitely delivered. The only thing I asked him for; was to take the sadness and anxiety away. I said I will handle the rest: and he did.

I thought I was broken but my angel Nancy Ellis pointed out that I wasn't broken, and that many of my colleagues tried to break me. Guess what? I am not broken. I am still standing. Now I can be a voice for others, so they do not have to go through what I went through. No one should have to endure the disrespect, humiliation, physical, mental and emotional abuse.

If I went through it, as a New York City Correction Officer, and currently experiencing it, visiting my nephew, in New York State Correctional facilities. You can only imagine what prisoners/inmates are going through in prison.

Many of my colleagues will probably be disturbed because I am revealing the insider secrets, facts and the truth. Yes, there is a blue wall of silence. However, why should I honor the blue wall of silence when all it did was, try to make my life a living hell?

What I want people to get from my book is reality and facts;

The individuals on Rikers Island have only been accused of a crime, not convicted. Until they had their day in court in front of a Judge and Jury; stop judging and casting doubt on people.

In conclusion; I will be here fighting for justice and disarming injustice. I don't know where this journey is going to take. It's an uphill systematic battle I intended to win.

God will show me the way and I will follow. Keep your eyes open and look out for Robin K. Miller. She is a force to be reckoned with.

ABOUT THE AUTHOR

Robin Kay Miller was born in Queens and raised in Brownsville Houses in Brooklyn NY. At the age of 22 she became a New York City Correction Officer on Rikers Island, in the Correctional Institution For Men , Formerly known as C-76. She worked at various institutions within the Correction Department. In 2005 she completed her 20 years of service and retired, with an impeccable record, and has since penned her memoirs.

She has appeared in WABC Channel 7" Nightline" CNN AC360 live with ANDERSON COOPER & CNN live with POPPY HARLOW and 77 WABC RADIO SAVAGE RADIO with DR. MICHAEL SAVAGE. She has a 2 page spread in the NYPOST by GARY BUISO.

She continues to embark on her career as a screenwriter and director of feature films. She plans to develops a movie and TV series about her experiences as a Correction Officer.

Made in the USA
Lexington, KY
25 February 2017